my first BAKING BOOK

my first BAKING BOOK

BY

Rena Coyle

ILLUSTRATED BY

Tedd Arnold

Workman Publishing
New York

Library of Congress Cataloging-in-Publication Data

Coyle, Rena. My first baking book.

    (Bialosky & friends) "100% loyal and true."
    Includes index.
    1. Pastry—Juvenile literature. I. Arnold, Tedd.
II. Title.   III. Series.
TX773.C635   1988   641.8′ 65   87-40646
ISBN 0-89480-579-7 (pbk.)

Cover and book design by Tedd Arnold

Workman books are available at special discounts
when purchased in bulk for premiums and sales
promotions as well as for fund-raising or educational
use. Special editions or book excerpts can also be
created to specification. For details, contact the
Special Sales Director at the address below.

Workman Publishing Company, Inc.
708 Broadway
New York, NY 10003

Printed in the United States of America

First printing July 1988
10 9 8 7

CONTENTS

To all my friends,

Hi! My name is Bialosky and I'm a great baker.

Baking with my friends and family is one of my favorite ways of sharing special treats and spending time together. Being able to make my own treats for holidays and special occasions gives me a wonderful feeling of accomplishment and good will.

I have chosen some of my favorite recipes for you. They are the same ones my grandmother and mother made for me over the years. But when I was growing up, we weren't as concerned about the amount of sugar we ate as we are today. Everyone still likes "sweets," but now we like them without all that sugar. So, I've reduced the amounts traditionally used in all these recipes and have still kept their good old-fashioned taste. Now my friends and I can have a cookie or two without thinking about how much sugar is in them.

The book is divided into sections so that it's easy for you to decide what to bake for any occasion. The sections range from breakfast bakes all the way to special extravaganzas. Try them all, and make sure you try my favorite chapter—Bearing Gifts. It dips into the honey jar.

So if it's your turn to bring in the school snack, or you need a dessert for the holiday dinner, or you are just in the mood to bake, put on your apron, talk it over with your parents, and get started!

Have fun! Bialosky

GETTING STARTED

BEFORE YOU BEGIN

1. Choose a recipe you would like to make, then ask an adult to read it through with you. Ask any questions you might have about the ingredients or steps.

Because you will be working with hot ovens and, in some cases, on top of the stove, an adult assistant must be available to help you. Make sure this fits in with the adult's plans, too. If you haven't spent much time in the kitchen and aren't familiar with the equipment (knives, electric mixers, and whatnot), you will want an adult there to show you the ropes. If you're an old pro at baking, you will still need a little help with difficult steps, such as unmolding a cake or taking a large pan out of the oven. Talk it over with your adult help.

2. Once you've chosen a recipe, check to see that you have all the ingredients. In some cases you will have to plan ahead and make a trip to the store or add a few items to the household shopping list.

3. Also check to see that you have the utensils and baking pans you need. If you don't have the correct size pan, choose a pan as close as possible to the size you need. You can even use two much smaller pans instead. If the pan is about the size you need, the baking time will be about the same. But if the pan size is very different, the baking time will be very different too.

4. When you are ready to begin, put on comfortable clothes and wear an apron. Roll up long sleeves and tie back long hair.

5. Clear a work space for yourself by putting away anything you are not going to use for your recipe. Accidents happen when you don't give yourself room to work.

6. Before handling food, wash your hands, rinse them, and then dry thoroughly. You are now ready to begin.

SAFETY FIRST

1. All the recipes in this book are baked in the oven. Instructions are given for the average gas or electric models that most people have in their homes, *not* for microwaves or convection ovens.

2. Gas ovens: Newer model gas ovens are self-lighting. You just turn the oven temperature dial to the heat you want and the oven will come on and heat up. Older gas ovens need to be lighted with a match. If your oven is this type, ask your adult assistant to light it for you. *Never light a gas oven with a match by yourself.*

3. Electric ovens: To heat an electric oven, you need only turn the temperature dial to the correct heat. This is true for all models.

4. Preheating an oven to the correct temperature before baking your recipe is important. It usually takes about 15 minutes for an oven to heat to the temperature you need. In each recipe, you are reminded to turn the oven on about 15 minutes before you will bake your recipe.

5. Not all ovens heat to the exact temperature set on the dial. Some are too hot and others too cool. An oven thermometer will tell you if the oven you are using is heating to the correct temperature. If you don't have one, ask an adult who uses the oven if you need to make any adjustments to get the temperature you need.

6. When checking or removing a pan from the oven, always pull the rack slightly out first. Don't reach deep into a hot oven to get a pan.

Make sure you have either a cooling rack or a hot pad nearby on which to place the hot baking pan. Never put a hot pan directly on a counter or table—it may burn the surface.

7. Always keep oven mitts and pot holders handy at the stove. Anytime you open the oven door or reach for a hot saucepan on top of the stove, you should have your oven mitts on.

8. When cooking on top of the stove, turn the handles of the saucepans you are using in toward the back of the stove. This will prevent anyone from accidentally bumping a hot pan and turning it over.

9. Some of these recipes call for a sharp knife. Always pick the knife up by the handle—not the blade—and work on a clean, dry cutting board. If you're chopping or slicing fruit that's been rinsed, dry it first so that it doesn't slip out of your hand. If cutting with the knife is not going smoothly, ask for help from your adult assistant.

10. Whenever you use an electric appliance (a blender, mixer, or food processor), make sure your hands are clean and dry before you plug it in. When you have finished with the appliance, unplug it (with dry hands). It's very important to use appliances carefully. Do not put your fingers or any utensils into a blender or food processor or mixer bowl when the machine is on. The appliance must be completely stopped before you scrape the sides of mixer bowl clean or take the cover off the blender or food processor.

11. Turn the oven or stove burners off as soon as you finish with them.

CLEAN UP

If you leave the kitchen clean, with all the utensils and ingredients in their place, you will be invited back to cook. Rinse and stack bowls, pans, and utensils in the sink as you go along and you will keep your workspace clear of clutter and make the job of cleaning up later that much easier.

COOKING PROCEDURES

Measuring
There are two kinds of measures—liquid and dry. Liquid measures are clear glass or plastic so that you can see the markings on the side and the liquid on the inside. Dry measures are a group of cups that measure from as little as 2 tablespoons or ¼ cup to 1 cup. Using the right amount of an ingredient is very important.

1. To measure dry ingredients, scoop up the full amount of the ingredient (usually flour and sugar) and then with the back of a table knife, scrape off the excess so that the measure is perfectly level.

2. To measure liquid, put the measuring cup on a counter and find the marking for the amount you need. Pour in the liquid up to that mark. Look at it at eye level to make sure it comes up to the mark and not above or below it.

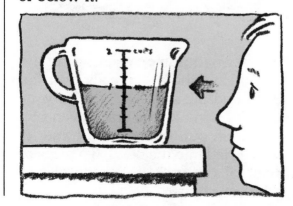

How to Tell When a Recipe Is Done

All these recipes tell you what the cake or cookies or pie will look like when it's done. To check, put your oven mitts on, pull the rack out slightly, and look carefully. If you're not sure, ask the opinion of your adult assistant.

How to Crack an Egg

1. Hold the egg in one hand and tap the middle of the shell, gently but firmly, against the rim of a bowl until it cracks.

2. Place a thumb on each side of the crack. Hold the egg directly over the bowl and push in lightly with your thumbs to make the crack even bigger. Then pull the egg apart and let the egg fall into the bowl. If a piece of shell falls in with it, just pull it out with your finger.

3. It doesn't matter if the yolk breaks unless the recipe calls for just egg yolks or egg whites. To keep the yolk from breaking, hold the egg close to where it will fall and gently crack the egg and separate it.

How to Separate an Egg

1. Put a wide-mesh strainer in a bowl. Carefully crack the egg into the strainer.

2. Lift the strainer and let the white drip through the holes into the bowl.

3. Pour the yolk into a different bowl.

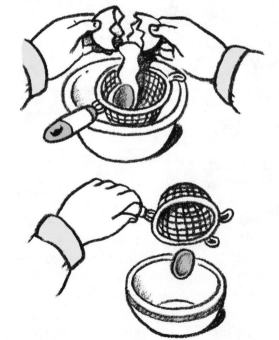

How to Whip Egg Whites

Egg whites whip best if they are at room temperature, so take the eggs out of the refrigerator and let them warm up before you need them. Before you separate the eggs, make sure that the mixing bowl is clean and dry. When you separate the eggs, none of the yolk should get mixed in with the whites.

1. Beat the egg whites first on medium speed until they are foamy.

2. Increase the speed to medium-high and continue to beat until the whites look like fluffy white clouds. Turn the mixer off.

3. If the fluffy peaks stand without falling, the whites are finished. But if the peaks start to fall in on themselves, you will have to beat them longer. Try to beat them until they are stiff enough to hold their shape but no longer.

11

How to Whip Cream

Pour cold heavy or whipping cream into a mixer bowl and beat with an electric mixer on medium speed until the cream is thick and fluffy, about 3 minutes.

How to Fold a Batter

1. Put the lighter mixture (such as egg whites or whipped cream) on top of the heavier batter in a large bowl.

2. Using a rubber spatula, bring the heavier batter from the bottom up and over the lighter one.

Turn the bowl a little and do it again. Keep turning the bowl and bringing the batter at the bottom over the top until it's blended. Do this gently.

How to Roll Out Pastry

1. Sprinkle flour lightly on a clean kitchen counter or pastry board. Place the dough in the center of the flour and press it even with the heel of your hand. Dust a little flour over the top.

2. Place the rolling pin on the center of the dough and firmly roll it away from you.

3. Lift the dough and turn it a quarter turn.

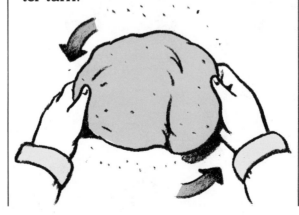

Put the rolling pin again on the center and roll the dough firmly away from you. Repeat this process of turning and rolling until the pastry is the size you want it to be.

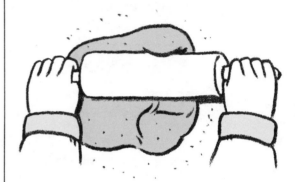

4. If the dough begins to stick, sprinkle a little more flour wherever it's sticking (under it or over it). If the edges start to crack, patch the cracks with your fingers and roll a little more lightly at the edges. When you get the pastry into the pie plate, you can always do more repairs with your fingers.

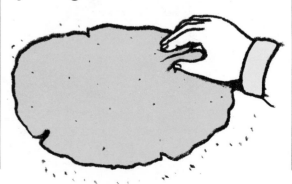

How to Line a Pie Plate with Pastry Dough

1. Roll up the pastry loosely on the rolling pin. Make sure it's not sticky or it will stick together. Pick up both ends of the pin and unroll it over the pie plate.

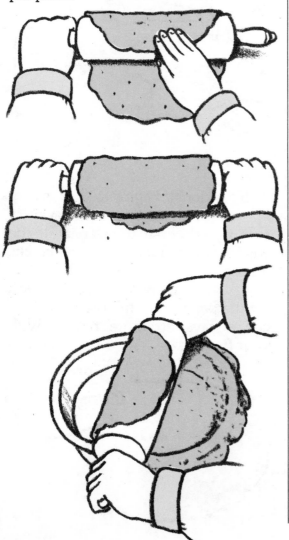

2. Or fold the dough in half to make a half circle, then in half again to make a quarter circle. Pick up the quarter circle, put the point in the middle of the pie plate, and unfold the dough.

3. Smooth out the dough with your hands and press it lightly on the bottom and sides of the dish.

4. Trim the dough that hangs over the edge with a knife or kitchen scissors.

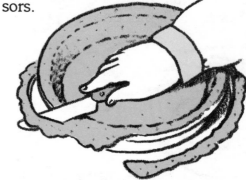

How to Knead Dough

1. Sprinkle a clean work surface lightly with flour and put a little extra flour off to the side.

2. Using your hands, lift the dough out of the bowl and put it on the floured surface.

3. Sprinkle all the sticky surfaces with a little more flour.

4. Put the heels of both hands in the center of the dough and push it away from you as far as you can.

5. Take that pushed-out edge and fold it over to meet the bottom edge.

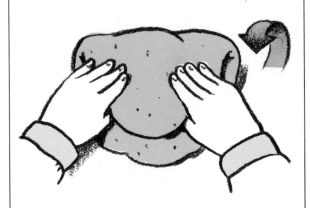

6. Pick up the dough and turn it a quarter turn.

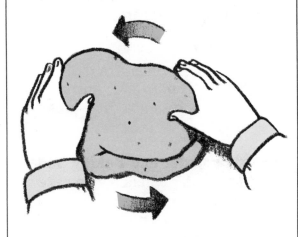

7. Repeat pushing the dough, folding it, and then turning it.

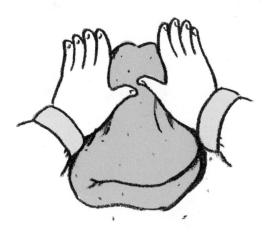

If the dough gets sticky, sprinkle a little more flour over it and under it. Don't add too much flour or the dough will be very stiff and hard to knead.

8. The dough is done when it is very springy, shiny, and smooth. It usually takes at least 5 minutes of continuous kneading. Recruit volunteers if you need them.

How to Grate

If you have a box grater, place it over a piece of waxed paper. Carefully grate in an up-and-down motion over the largest holes of the grater. Do this slowly, so that you don't scrape your knuckles. If you have a grater that doesn't stand by itself, place it over a mixing bowl or hold it up with one hand and grate with the other hand.

How to Sift Confectioner's Sugar

Put a tablespoon of sugar in a small tea strainer or sieve. Holding the strainer over the cake, gently tap the sides of the strainer with your fingers. The sugar will float down over the cake like snow.

WHAT ABOUT INGREDIENTS USED IN BAKING?

Eggs
Brown and white eggs are exactly alike. All of these recipes were tested with large eggs.

Milk and Cream
Milk varies by fat content. All of our recipes were tested with whole milk. You can substitute skim, 1%, or 2% for it, but it will change the texture of the finished cake or cookie a little. Using skim milk will make the big- gest difference and 2% the least.

Don't substitute light cream or half-and-half for heavy cream (also called whipping cream).

Yeast
Yeast is a living organism that grows when mixed with flour and liquid. Bread rises because the yeast is growing.

Baking Powder and Baking Soda
Baking powder will lighten a cake or cookie batter. Baking soda makes the texture of a cake or cookie tender; it is used when a batter has lemon, spices, honey, or molasses in it. Both baking powder and soda get stale after about six months and should be replaced with a new supply.

Spices
Most spices come in two forms— whole and ground. Nearly all baking recipes use ground spices. Spices are very strong and must be measured carefully. To do this, put the measuring spoon in the box or bottle and scoop up all you can so that the spoon is overflowing. Then scrape off the extra with a knife or against the opening in the can so that the spice is even with the top of the spoon. If there's a spice you really don't like, you can substitute other spices for it.

Cooking Apples
The most popular apples for cooking are Golden Delicious, Granny Smith, McIntosh, Cortland, and Rome.

BREAKFAST BAKING

SPICED APPLE MUFFINETTES • FRUIT-FILLED POCKETS • BAKED APPLE DUMPLING • PEACH CRISP • BAKED DOUGHNUT NUGGETS • BREAKFAST BREAD WITH OATMEAL STREUSEL • OATMEAL BREAKFAST CAKE • POWER BARS • BAKED APPLE PANCAKE

Spiced Apple Muffinettes

Preparation time: 35 minutes
Baking time: 20 minutes for miniature muffins; 30 minutes for regular muffins
Makes: 24 miniature muffins or 12 regular muffins

These miniature muffins are great to serve at a honey bear tea as well as your breakfast. If you're crazy about nuts and raisins, sprinkle a tablespoon of each into the batter—they make great additions.

INGREDIENTS

- ½ cup (1 stick) butter, plus 1 tablespoon for the pans, at room temperature
- 1 medium apple
- ½ cup sugar
- 2 large eggs
- ⅓ cup milk
- 1¾ cups all-purpose flour
- 1 tablespoon baking powder
- 2 teaspoons ground cinnamon
- 2 teaspoons ground ginger
- ½ cup unsweetened applesauce

UTENSILS

Paper towel • Two 12-cup miniature muffin tins or one 12-cup regular muffin tin • Cutting board • Vegetable peeler • Knife • Teaspoon • Measuring cups and spoons • Mixer bowl • Electric mixer • Rubber spatula • Spoon • Oven mitts • Cooling rack

1 Place an oven rack in the center of the oven. Then turn on the oven and preheat to 350°F. Using the paper towel, spread the 1 tablespoon of butter evenly in the muffin cups.

2 Put the apple on the cutting board. Holding the apple steady, peel the skin off the apple with the

vegetable peeler. Carefully cut the apple in half through the stem end and center of the core. Holding each half in the palm of your hand, scoop out the seeds and core with a teaspoon or metal teaspoon measure.

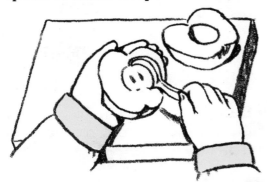

Turn the apple halves cut side down on the cutting board. Cut the apple into thin slices, then cut across the slices several times to roughly chop it. Set the apple aside.

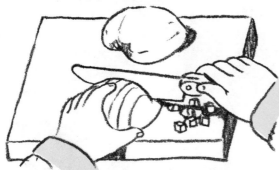

3 Put the butter and sugar in the mixer bowl. Using the electric mixer, beat until the mixture looks creamy and pale yellow. Break the

eggs into the butter mixture and beat until completely blended. Pour the milk into the batter and mix until smooth.

4 Mix in the flour a spoonful at a time, then mix in the baking powder, cinnamon, and ginger.

5 Add the apple chunks and applesauce and stir with the rubber spatula.

6 Spoon the batter evenly into the muffin cups.

7 Put on the oven mitts and put the tins in the oven. Bake miniature muffins for 20 minutes and regular muffins for 30 minutes. The muffins are done when the tops have puffed and turned golden brown.

8 Wearing your mitts, carefully transfer the tins to the cooling rack. Let the muffins cool for 10 minutes. Put the oven mitts back on and turn the tins upside down on the rack to remove the muffins.

Fruit-Filled Pockets

Preparation time: 35 minutes
Baking time: 20 minutes
Makes: 10 filled biscuits

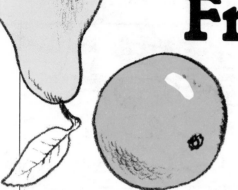

Fill these pockets with pear pieces, banana slices and nuts, or any fresh fruit combination. They make a delicious beginning to any day.

INGREDIENTS

1 medium pear

4 tablespoons (½ stick) butter

2½ cups all-purpose flour, plus ½ cup for rolling out the dough

1 tablespoon baking powder

½ teaspoon ground cloves

½ teaspoon salt

1 cup milk

1 large egg

1 tablespoon water

½ cup orange marmalade or juice-sweetened jam

UTENSILS

Cutting board • Knife • Small saucepan • Measuring cups and spoons • Oven mitts • Large and small mixing bowls • Wooden spoon • Rolling pin • Ruler • 3-inch round cookie cutter • Cookie sheet • Fork • Metal spatula

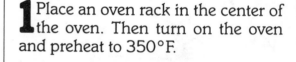

1 Place an oven rack in the center of the oven. Then turn on the oven and preheat to 350°F.

2 Put the pear on the cutting board. Holding the pear steady, peel the skin off the pear with the vegetable peeler. Carefully cut the pear in half through the stem end and center of the core. Holding each half in the palm of your hand, scoop out the seeds and core with a teaspoon or metal teaspoon measure.

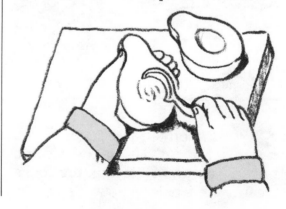

Turn the pear halves cut side down on the cutting board. Cut the pear into thin slices, then cut across the slices several times to roughly chop it. Set the pear aside.

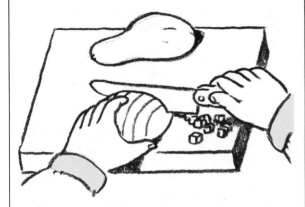

3 Place the butter in the small saucepan and set the pan over medium heat. Heat the butter until half of it is melted, then turn the heat off, put on the oven mitts and move the pan to a heatproof surface.

4 Place 2½ cups flour, the baking powder, cloves, and salt in the mixing bowl and stir together with the wooden spoon.

Pour in the milk and the butter (it will be completely melted by this time) and stir until blended.

5 Sprinkle a clean kitchen surface with about ¼ cup flour. Place the dough on the floured surface and gently even it out with your hands. Sprinkle a little more flour over the top. Using the rolling pin, roll out the dough ½ inch thick (see page 11).

Dip the cookie cutter into flour and press it into the dough to cut circles.

Arrange the circles on the cookie sheet. Stack the scraps on top of each other, press together lightly, and roll out. Cut out as many more circles as you can.

6 Break the egg into the small bowl. Add 1 tablespoon water and stir with the fork until blended.

Dip your finger into the egg, and dab the egg around the edge of each circle.

7 Spoon a generous teaspoon of marmalade on the center of each circle.

Using your fingers, break the pears into small chunks (about ½ inch big) and place 1 or 2 pieces on the marmalade. Fold each biscuit in half, making sure the edges meet. Using the fork, press the edges together.

8 Put on the oven mitts and put the cookie sheet in the oven. Bake until the biscuits are golden brown, about 20 minutes.

9 Wearing your mitts, carefully transfer the cookie sheet to a heatproof surface. Let the biscuits cool 10 minutes before transferring them to a plate with the spatula.

Did You Know?

The word biscuit means twice-cooked bread. Originally biscuits were baked, then split in half, and baked again until they were hard and dry, which made them longer lasting and easier to carry on long journeys.

Baked Apple Dumpling

Preparation time: 60 minutes
Baking time: 40 minutes
Makes: 6 servings

Any occasion is the right one for these pastry-covered filled apple halves. Serve them with a spoonful of vanilla yogurt for a very special breakfast or with a scoop of ice cream for dessert.

INGREDIENTS

DOUGH:

2 cups all-purpose flour plus ¼ cup for rolling out the dough

2 tablespoons sugar

½ teaspoon salt

½ teaspoon ground nutmeg

¾ cup vegetable shortening

4 to 5 tablespoons cold water

APPLES and FILLING:

2 tablespoons butter, at room temperature

¾ teaspoon ground cinnamon

1½ cups chopped walnuts

3 medium apples

UTENSILS

Large and small mixing bowls • Measuring cups and spoons • Fork • Plastic wrap • Cutting board • Vegetable peeler • Utility knife • Teaspoon • 9-inch square or round baking pan • Rolling pin • Oven mitts • Cooling rack

1 Make the dough: Place 2 cups flour, the sugar, salt, and nutmeg in the large mixing bowl and stir together with the fork. Add the shortening and rub the flour and shortening together between your fingertips until all the shortening disappears into the flour.

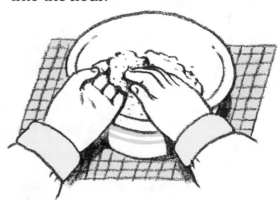

2 Sprinkle the flour mixture all over with 4 tablespoons water and stir with the fork until the water is evenly distributed. Press the

dough together with your hands; if it doesn't stick together, sprinkle on 1 more tablespoon water. Now press the dough with the heels of your hands to make it smooth.

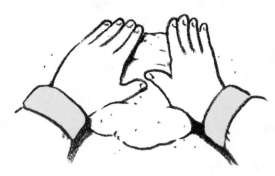

Shape the dough into a flattened ball and wrap in a piece of plastic wrap. Refrigerate it while you prepare the apples and filling.

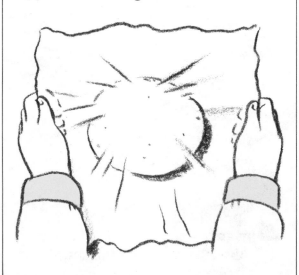

3 Put the butter and cinnamon in the small bowl. Using your fingers, work them together into a paste. Add the nuts and mix until blended. Set the filling aside.

4 Put the apples on the cutting board. Holding the apple steady, peel the skin off each apple with the vegetable peeler.

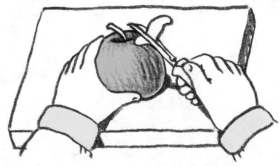

Carefully cut each apple in half through the stem end and center of the core. Holding each half in the

palm of your hand, scoop out the seeds and core with the teaspoon or metal teaspoon measure.

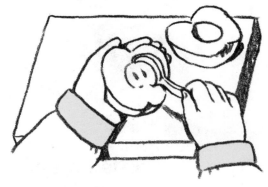

5 Place the apples, cut side up, in the baking pan. They should all fit in a single layer. Put a spoonful of the nut mixture in the hollow of each apple half. Put any extra nut mixture around the apples.

6 Place an oven rack in the center of the oven. Then turn on the oven and preheat to 350°F.

7 Sprinkle a clean kitchen surface with a little flour. Unwrap the dough and put it on the floured surface. Flatten the dough with your fingers and sprinkle a little flour over the top.

8 Using the rolling pin, roll out the dough ¼ inch thick (see page 11). Very loosely roll the dough on the

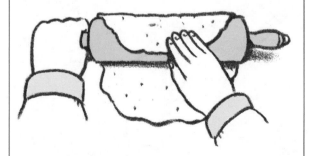

rolling pin, then unroll it over the apples. If the dough tears, just pinch it together with your fingers.

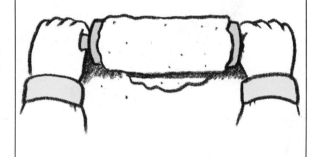

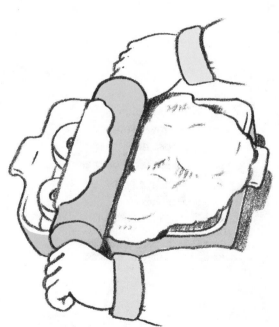

Gently press the dough over the apples. Trim off any extra dough that hangs over the sides of the pan.

9 Put on the oven mitts and put the baking pan in the oven. Bake for 40 minutes.

10 Wearing the mitts, carefully transfer the pan to the cooling rack. Let the apples cool for 20 minutes before spooning them out to eat.

Peach Crisp

Preparation time: 25 minutes
Baking time: 30 minutes
Makes: 6 servings

Perfect for breakfast with a pitcher of milk alongside.

INGREDIENTS

1 can (32 ounces) unsweetened peach slices, drained, or 5 fresh peaches, peeled, pitted, and sliced (see Tip)

2 tablespoons tapioca

¾ teaspoon ground cinnamon

¼ teaspoon ground cloves

¾ cup (1½ sticks) butter

2 tablespoons brown sugar

¾ cup all-purpose flour

1½ cups quick-cooking oatmeal

UTENSILS

Large mixing bowl • Measuring cups and spoons • Wooden spoon • Rubber spatula • 9-inch ovenproof skillet • Medium-size saucepan • Oven mitts • Cooling rack

1 Place an oven rack in the center of the oven. Then turn on the oven and preheat to 350°F.

2 Place the peach slices (you should have about 3 cups) in the mixing bowl. Add the tapioca, ¼ teaspoon cinnamon, and the cloves

and stir gently with the wooden spoon. Scrape the peaches into the skillet.

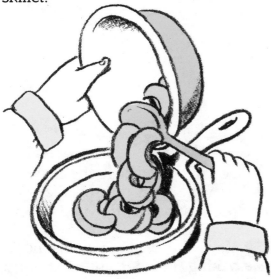

3 Put the butter in the saucepan and place it over medium heat. Heat the butter until half of it is melted. Turn off the heat. Put on the oven mitts and transfer the pan to a heatproof surface.

Add the brown sugar and stir until smooth. Add the flour, oatmeal, and remain-

ing ½ teaspoon cinnamon and stir together. Spoon the topping over the peaches and press it lightly onto the peaches with your hand.

4 Put on the oven mitts and put the skillet in the oven. Bake until the topping is lightly browned, about 30 minutes.

5 Wearing the mitts, carefully transfer the skillet to the cooling rack. Let the crisp cool slightly before dishing it up. If you like, serve it with vanilla yogurt, cream, or milk.

Tip: If you make this with fresh peaches, peel the skin off using a vegetable peeler. Then cut the peaches in half and twist the halves apart. Pull out the pit with your fingers and cut each peach half into slices.

Did You Know?
The peach came to America from halfway around the world. Explorers brought the peach from China to Europe, then from Europe the peach traveled with the settlers to America.

Baked Doughnut Nuggets

Preparation time: 25 minutes
Baking time: 20 minutes
Makes: 30 nuggets

Traditionally doughnuts are fried in oil, but these are baked instead, so they are not heavy or greasy. Have them plain or dusted lightly with cinnamon sugar.

INGREDIENTS

BATTER:

1 ½ cups all-purpose flour
2 teaspoons baking powder
1 teaspoon ground nutmeg
½ teaspoon salt
½ cup (1 stick) butter, at room
  temperature
⅓ cup sugar
1 large egg
⅔ cup milk

OPTIONAL TOPPING:

2 tablespoons confectioner's sugar
¼ teaspoon ground cinnamon

UTENSILS

Measuring cups and spoons • Medium-size mixing bowl • Mixer bowl • Electric mixer • Rubber spatula • Spoon • 2 or 3 miniature muffin tins (30 cups) • Oven mitts • Medium-size saucepan • Shallow bowl • Cooling racks

1 Place an oven rack in the center of the oven. Then turn on the oven and preheat to 350°F.

2 Make the batter: Put the flour, baking powder, nutmeg, and salt in the medium-size mixing bowl and stir them together with your fingers.

3 Put the butter and sugar in the mixer bowl. Using the electric mixer, beat on medium-high speed until light and fluffy.

Stop every once in a while to scrape the sides of the bowl clean with the rubber spatula.

4 Break the egg into the bowl and beat until completely blended.

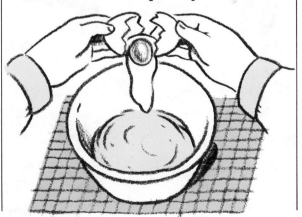

5 Add half the flour mixture and mix on low speed until smooth. Stop the mixer, pour in half the milk, and mix again until smooth.

6 Add the remaining flour mixture and mix until blended. Then add the remaining milk and mix again until smooth.

7 Using the spoon, fill each muffin cup two-thirds full with batter.

8 Put the oven mitts on and put the tins in the oven. Bake 20 minutes.

9 Put the confectioner's sugar and cinnamon in the bowl and stir them together with your fingers.

10 Wearing the mitts, carefully transfer the pans to the cooling racks. Let the nuggets cool 5 minutes, then put the oven mitts back on and turn the tins on their sides, letting the nuggets fall out.

11 Serve the nuggets plain or lightly sprinkle the tops with the cinnamon sugar.

Breakfast Bread with Oatmeal Streusel

Preparation time: 45 minutes   Baking time: 1 hour 10 minutes   Makes: 1 loaf

The crunchy oatmeal crust makes this bread special. It's perfect for a late weekend breakfast—bake it Saturday, wrap it in plastic, and refrigerate it until Sunday morning.

INGREDIENTS

TOPPING:

2 tablespoons butter, at room temperature

2 tablespoons honey

⅔ cup oatmeal

½ cup walnut pieces

½ teaspoon ground cinnamon

BREAD BATTER:

3 tablespoons butter, plus 2 teaspoons for the pan, at room temperature

1 cup all-purpose flour

¼ cup oatmeal

2 teaspoons baking powder

1 teaspoon ground cinnamon

¼ cup (packed) brown sugar

1 large egg

1 cup milk

1 cup walnut pieces

UTENSILS

Measuring cups and spoons • Mixer bowl • Electric mixer • Rubber spatula • 2 small mixing bowls • Plastic wrap • Paper towel • 9 x 5-inch loaf pan • Oven mitts • Cooling rack

1 Make the topping: Put the butter and honey in the mixer bowl. Using the electric mixer, beat on medium speed until smooth.

Add the oatmeal, walnuts, and cinnamon; mix on low speed until blended.

Scrape the streusel topping into a small bowl, cover the bowl with plastic wrap, and set it aside.

2 Place an oven rack in the center of the oven. Then turn on the oven and preheat to 350°F.

3 Using the paper towel, spread the 2 teaspoons of butter evenly over the bottom and sides of the loaf pan.

4 Make the bread batter: Put the flour, oatmeal, baking powder, and cinnamon in the second small mixing bowl and stir them together with your fingers or a fork.

5 Wash and dry the mixer bowl and beater. Put the 3 tablespoons of butter and the brown sugar in the bowl. Using the electric mixer, beat on medium speed until smooth.

6 Break the egg into the butter mixture and beat until completely blended.

7 Add half the flour mixture and mix on low speed until smooth.

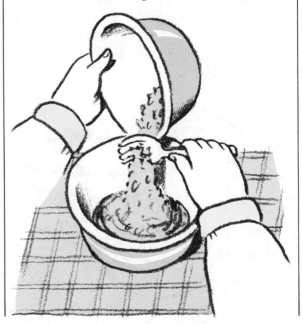

Add half the milk and mix again until blended. Add the rest of the flour mixture, then blend in the remaining milk. The batter should be nice and smooth.

Add the walnuts and mix until the nuts are evenly distributed through the batter. Stop every once in a while to scrape the sides of the bowl clean with the rubber spatula.

8 Scrape the batter into the prepared pan and spread evenly.

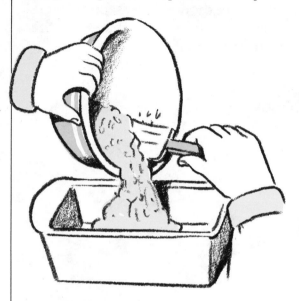

9 Sprinkle the streusel topping over the batter.

10 Put the oven mitts on and put the pan in the oven. Bake until the bread pulls away from the sides of the pan, 1 hour to 1 hour 10 minutes.

11 Wearing the mitts, carefully transfer the pan to the cooling rack. Let cool for 10 minutes.

Then put the mitts back on and tilt the pan, letting the bread fall out onto the rack. Turn the bread right side up and let it cool at least 15 minutes before slicing it. Or cool completely, wrap in plastic wrap, and refrigerate until serving time.

31

Oatmeal Breakfast Cake

Preparation time: 20 minutes
Baking time: 40 minutes
Makes: 6 servings

Here's a breakfast cereal you can cut into squares and eat with a fork.

INGREDIENTS

1 teaspoon butter
1½ cups quick-cooking oatmeal (not instant)
2 cups milk
½ cup all-purpose flour
1½ teaspoons baking powder
½ teaspoon ground cinnamon
¼ cup sugar
2 large eggs
1 cup walnut pieces
½ cup raisins
Honey, low-fat yogurt, and fresh fruit, for serving

UTENSILS

Paper towel • 8-inch round baking pan • Measuring cups and spoons • Large mixing bowl • Wooden spoon • Rubber spatula • Oven mitts • Cookie sheet • Cooling Rack • Knife

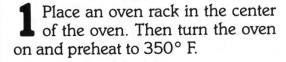

1 Place an oven rack in the center of the oven. Then turn the oven on and preheat to 350° F.

2 Using the paper towel, spread the butter evenly over the bottom and side of the baking pan.

3 Place the oatmeal in the mixing bowl and stir in the milk with the wooden spoon. Let the mixture rest for 2 to 3 minutes. The oatmeal should absorb some of the milk. Add the flour, baking powder, cinnamon, and sugar, then stir until the batter is well blended.

4 Break the eggs into the bowl and stir them into the batter.

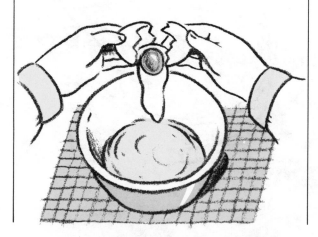

5 Stir the walnuts and raisins into the batter so that they are well mixed.

6 Pour the batter into the prepared baking pan, scraping the bowl clean with the rubber spatula.

7 Put on the oven mitts and place the cookie sheet in the oven. Put the baking pan on the cookie sheet and bake until the top of the cake has formed a golden crust, about 40 minutes.

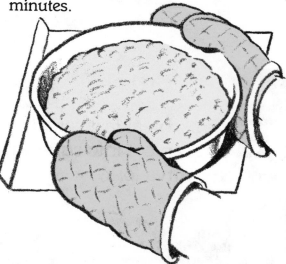

8 Transfer the cake to the cooling rack. Cool for 10 minutes before cutting. Serve the cake warm with honey, yogurt, and fruit.

Power Bars

Preparation time: 20 minutes
Baking time: 20 minutes
Makes: 12 bars

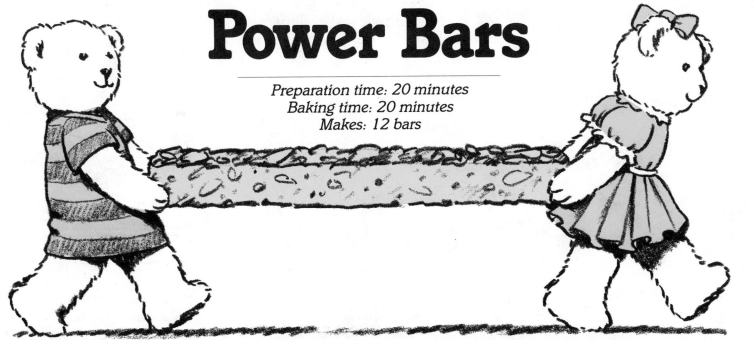

These bars make good traveling companions. Keep a couple wrapped up in your pocket or schoolbag. That way you'll be prepared when you and a friend have a "hungry" attack.

INGREDIENTS

¾ cup (1½ sticks) butter, plus 2 teaspoons for the pan, at room temperature

⅓ cup (packed) brown sugar

¼ cup all-purpose flour

1 teaspoon vanilla extract

5 cups unsweetened granola

UTENSILS

Paper towel • 9-inch square baking pan • Small saucepan • Oven mitts • Large mixing bowl • Measuring cups and spoons • Wooden spoon • Cooling rack • Knife • Metal spatula

1 Place an oven rack in the center of the oven. Then turn on the oven and preheat to 375°F.

2 Using a paper towel, spread the 2 teaspoons of butter evenly over the bottom and sides of the baking pan.

3 Put ¾ cup butter in the small saucepan. Heat over medium heat just until the butter is melted.

Turn off the heat, put on the oven mitts, and carefully pour it into the mixing bowl.

4 Add the brown sugar, flour, and vanilla to the butter and stir thoroughly with the wooden spoon.

5 Add the granola and stir very well to coat all the granola with the butter mixture. When you think it is completely mixed, check the bottom of the bowl one more time.

6 Spoon the granola into the prepared baking pan. Press it flat using the back of the spoon or your hands.

7 Put the oven mitts on and put the pan in the oven. Bake until the top is golden brown, 15 to 20 minutes.

8 Wearing the mitts, carefully transfer the pan to the cooling rack. Let it cool completely, at least 30 minutes, before cutting it.

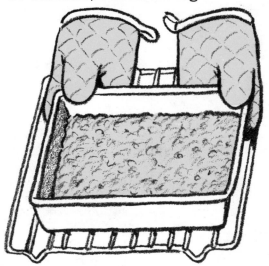

9 Using the knife, cut the granola into 4 strips lengthwise and 4 strips crosswise. Remove the bars from the pan with the metal spatula.

Tip: If you like your bars crisper, bake them 5 minutes longer the next time you make them. If your bars are getting too crisp, bake them 3 minutes less.

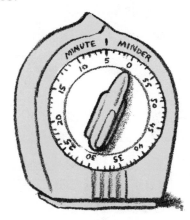

Baked Apple Pancake

Preparation time: 25 minutes
Baking time: 25 minutes
Makes: 6 servings

This pancake bakes in the oven and comes out high and fluffy. As it cools, it falls. Add a spoonful of yogurt and enjoy it at breakfast or brunch.

INGREDIENTS

2 tablespoons butter, at room temperature, plus 1 teaspoon for the cake pan

1 medium apple

2 tablespoons sugar

¼ teaspoon ground cinnamon

2 large eggs

½ cup milk

½ cup all-purpose flour

Low-fat yogurt (optional)

UTENSILS

Paper towel • 9-inch cake pan • Cutting board • Vegetable peeler • Knife • Teaspoon • Mixer bowl • Measuring cups and spoons • Wooden spoon • Electric mixer • Oven mitts • Hot pad

1 Place an oven rack in the center of the oven. Then turn on the oven and preheat to 400°F.

2 Using the paper towel, spread the 1 teaspoon of butter generously over the bottom and sides of the cake pan.

3 Put the apple on the cutting board. Holding the apple steady, peel the skin off with the vegetable peeler.

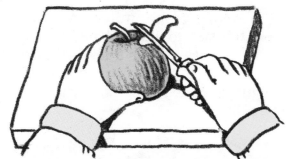

Carefully cut the apple in half through the stem end and center of the core. Holding each apple half in the palm of your hand, scoop out the seeds and core with a teaspoon or metal teaspoon measure.

Turn the apple halves cut side down on the cutting board and cut into thin slices. Put the slices in the mixer bowl.

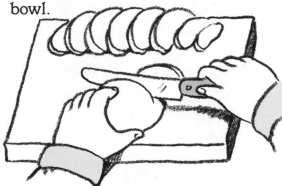

4 Add the sugar and cinnamon to the apple and stir with the wooden spoon until the slices are evenly coated with sugar. Spread the apple in the prepared cake pan.

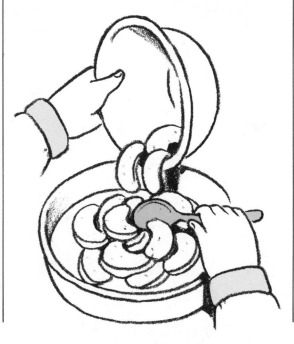

5 Break the eggs into the mixer bowl (don't bother to wash the bowl first). Using the electric mixer, beat on medium speed until they are blended. Pour in the milk and beat again until blended.

6 With the mixer running on low speed, mix in the flour 1 tablespoon at a time.

7 Pour the batter over the apples. Cut the remaining 2 tablespoons of butter into little pieces and sprinkle them over the batter.

8 Put on the oven mitts and put the pan in the oven. Bake until the pancake is very puffy and has pulled away slightly from the sides of the pan, 25 minutes.

9 Wearing the mitts, carefully transfer to the hot pad on the table. Let it cool for a few minutes. Serve the pancake warm, with a little yogurt spooned over each serving if you like.

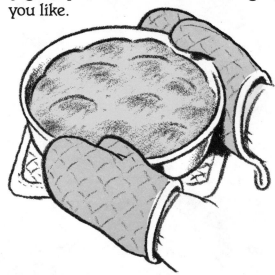

BEARING GIFTS

HONEY KISSES • HONEY LEMON BARS • HONEY 'N' SPICE BITS • HONEY GRAHAMS

Honey Kisses

Preparation time: 30 minutes
Total baking time: 24 minutes
Makes: 36 cookies

Bake these when your friends are around because they are at their best while warm.

INGREDIENTS

2 ¼ cups all-purpose flour

1 tablespoon baking soda

1 teaspoon ground cinnamon

½ teaspoon ground cloves

¾ cup (1 ½ sticks) butter, at room temperature

⅓ cup honey

2 tablespoons granulated sugar

1 large egg

1 cup coarsely chopped pecans

UTENSILS

Measuring cups and spoons • Medium-size mixing bowl • Mixer bowl • Electric mixer • 2 cookie sheets • Oven mitts • Cooling rack

1 Place an oven rack in the center of the oven. Then turn on the oven and preheat to 350°F.

2 Put the flour, baking soda, cinnamon, and cloves in the mixing bowl and stir them together with your fingers or a fork.

3 Put the butter, honey, and granulated sugar in the mixer bowl. Using the electric mixer, beat on high speed until smooth and creamy.

4 Break the egg into the butter mixture and beat until blended.

5 Add the flour mixture, half at a time, and mix on low speed until blended after each addition.

6 Add the pecans and mix just until they are evenly distributed through the dough.

7 Pinch off a piece of dough and roll it between your palms into a ball about as big as a quarter. Put the ball on a cookie sheet. Repeat with the remaining dough, placing the balls about 1 inch apart on the sheet, until the sheet is filled.

8 Put the oven mitts on and put the cookie sheet in the oven. Bake for 12 minutes. The cookies are done when the tops crack slightly.

9 Meanwhile, shape the rest of the dough into balls and arrange them on the other cookie sheet.

10 Wearing the mitts, carefully transfer the sheet of baked cookies to the cooling rack. Bake the second sheet of cookies.

Honey Lemon Bars

Preparation time: 25 minutes
Baking time: 40 minutes
Makes: 16 bars

These sweet-tart bars will fast become a favorite. They make the perfect snack to serve to your friends at a play-date or party. Serve them with mugs of hot apple cider or juice.

INGREDIENTS

DOUGH:
1 cup all-purpose flour
2 tablespoons sugar
½ cup (1 stick) butter, cold

FILLING:
2 large eggs
¼ cup honey
3 tablespoons lemon juice
2 tablespoons all-purpose flour
½ teaspoon baking powder

UTENSILS

Measuring cups and spoons • Large and medium-size mixing bowls • Knife • 8-inch square baking pan • Oven mitts • Whisk • Cooling rack • Small metal spatula

1 Place an oven rack in the center of the oven. Then turn on the oven and preheat to 350°F.

2 Make the dough: Place the flour and sugar in the large mixing bowl and stir them together with your fingers.

Cut the butter into small pieces and sprinkle the bits over the flour. Rub the butter and flour together between your fingertips until all the butter disappears into the flour.

3 Gather the dough together and put it in the baking pan. Using your hands, press it evenly over the bottom of the pan.

4 Put the oven mitts on and put the pan in the oven. Bake for 12 minutes.

5 While the crust is baking, make the filling: Break the eggs into the medium-size mixing bowl. Add the honey and lemon juice and whisk until completely blended. Add the flour and baking powder and continue to whisk until smooth.

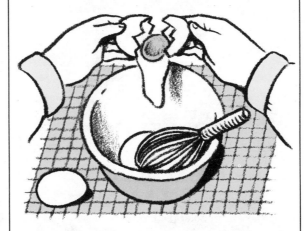

6 Wearing the mitts, carefully transfer the pan to a heatproof surface.

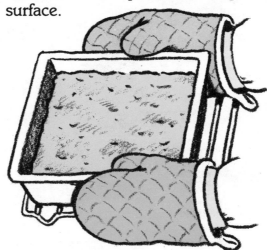

Pour the filling over the crust. Put the oven mitts back on and put the pan in the oven. Bake for 25 minutes. Put on the oven mitts, pull out the rack slightly, and shake the pan. If the filling is solid, the tart is done. If it is loose, bake another 5 minutes.

7 Transfer the pan to the cooling rack. Let it cool for 10 minutes, then cut the tart into bars. Use the spatula to take the bars out of the pan and put them on a plate.

Honey 'n' Spice Bits

Preparation time: 20 minutes   Baking time: 20 minutes   Makes: 24 bits

FOR SUZY
Love, Bialosky

Bake these flavorful little cupcakes in paper muffin tin liners. It will make them look party perfect at your next Teddy Bear tea.

INGREDIENTS

1½ cups all-purpose flour

1 teaspoon baking soda

1 teaspoon ground cinnamon

¼ teaspoon ground cloves

¼ teaspoon ground allspice

¼ cup (½ stick) butter, at room temperature

2 tablespoons brown sugar

⅓ cup honey

2 large eggs

½ cup low-fat yogurt

UTENSILS

2 miniature muffin tins (24 cups) • Paper liners to fit miniature cups • Measuring cups and spoons • Medium-size mixing bowl • Mixer bowl • Electric mixer • Rubber spatula • Spoon • Oven mitts • Cooling racks

1 Place an oven rack in the center of the oven. Then turn on the oven and preheat to 350°F. Line 24 muffin cups with paper liners.

2 Put the flour, baking soda, cinnamon, cloves, and allspice in the mixing bowl and stir them together with your fingers.

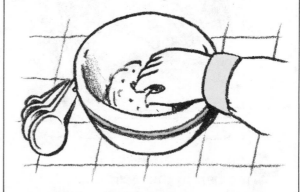

3 Put the butter and sugar in the mixer bowl. Using the electric mixer, beat on medium-high speed until light and fluffy. Stop every once in a while to scrape the sides of the bowl clean with the rubber spatula. Add the honey and beat until blended.

4 Break the eggs into the mixer bowl and beat on medium speed until completely blended.

5 Add half the flour mixture and mix on low speed until smooth.

Then add the yogurt and mix again until smooth. Add the remaining flour mixture and mix until smooth.

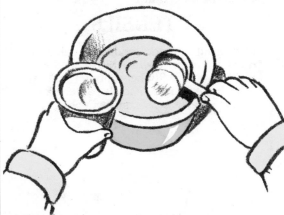

6 Using the spoon, fill each paper liner about three-quarters full with the batter.

7 Put the oven mitts on and put the tins in the oven. Bake until the tops are golden brown, about 20 minutes.

8 Wearing the mitts, carefully transfer the tins to the cooling rack. Let cool for about 10 minutes. Then put the mitts back on and turn each tin on its side, letting the honey bits fall out.

Tip: The batter can also be baked in regular muffin pans. They'll take about 30 minutes to bake.

Honey Grahams

Preparation time: 30 minutes
Total baking time: 20 minutes
Makes: 24 crackers

Honey grahams are spice-sweetened crackers that make great snacks to have along with a cold glass of milk.

INGREDIENTS

3 tablespoons sugar
1 teaspoon ground cinnamon
2 cups whole-wheat flour
½ teaspoon baking soda
¼ cup (½ stick) butter, at room temperature
¼ cup honey
½ cup heavy cream

UTENSILS

Measuring cups and spoons • Small and medium mixing bowls • Mixer bowl • Electric mixer • Rubber spatula • Rolling pin • Ruler • Knife • Metal spatula • 2 cookie sheets • Oven mitts • Cooling rack

1 Place an oven rack in the center of the oven. Then turn on the oven and preheat to 350°F.

2 Mix 1 tablespoon sugar and ½ teaspoon cinnamon in the small mixing bowl with your fingers or a fork; set aside.

3 Put 1½ cups flour, the baking soda, and remaining ½ teaspoon cinnamon in the medium bowl and stir them together with your fingers.

4 Put the butter, honey, and remaining 2 tablespoons sugar in the mixer bowl. Using the electric mixer, beat on medium speed until smooth and creamy.

Stop once or twice to scrape the sides of the bowl clean with the rubber spatula.

5 Add the flour mixture, half at a time, and mix on low speed until blended after each addition.

6 Pour in the cream and mix on low speed until the dough is smooth.

7 Sprinkle some of the remaining ½ cup flour over a clean kitchen surface. Turn the dough out of the bowl onto the floured surface and pat it flat with your hands. Sprinkle some more flour over the top and spread it with your hands.

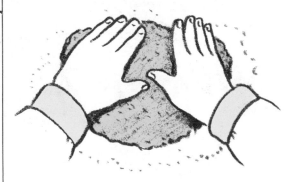

8 Using the rolling pin, roll out the dough ¼ inch thick (see page 11).

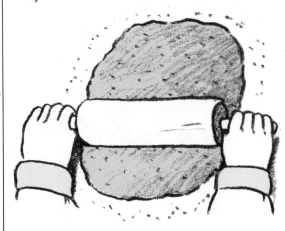

9 Using the ruler and the knife, cut the dough into 2½-inch squares.

Use the metal spatula to transfer the squares to the cookie sheets, placing them about 1½ inches apart.

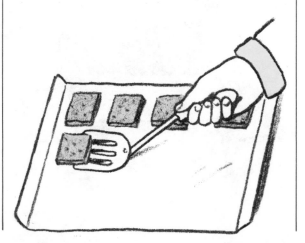

10 Put the oven mitts on and put a cookie sheet in the oven. Bake for 10 minutes.

11 Wearing the mitts, carefully transfer the cookie sheet to a heatproof surface. Bake the second sheet of crackers. While the crackers are cooling, sprinkle them with the cinnamon sugar that you set aside in Step 2. Let the crackers cool completely on the sheet. To keep the crackers crisp, store them in an airtight container.

Did you know?

The graham cracker was originally developed as a health food that was good for digestion. It was named for Sylvester Graham, a preacher and nutrition expert in the early 19th Century.

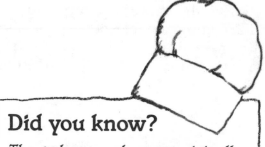

HOLIDAY SPECIALS

LINZER HEARTS • EASTER DAFFODIL CAKE • BAKED ALASKA • INDIAN PUDDING PIE •
• NOODLE PUDDING • SUGAR PLUM CAKE

Linzer Hearts

Preparation time: 35 minutes
Refrigeration time: 1 hour
Total baking time: 18 minutes
Makes: 12 hearts

There is nothing like giving your sweetheart a sweet heart for Valentine's Day.

INGREDIENTS

¾ cup pecan pieces

½ cup graham cracker crumbs (4 whole graham crackers)

1½ cups all-purpose flour, plus ½ cup for rolling out the dough

1 teaspoon baking powder

1 teaspoon ground cinnamon

¾ cup (1½ sticks) butter, at room temperature

¼ cup sugar

1 large egg

½ teaspoon vanilla extract

1 cup juice-sweetened raspberry jam

3 tablespoons water

UTENSILS

Measuring cups and spoons • Food processor or blender • 3 small mixing bowls • Mixer bowl • Electric mixer • Rubber spatula • Plastic wrap • Rolling pin • 2½-inch heart-shaped cookie cutter • Thin metal spatula • 2 cookie sheets • 1½-inch round cookie cutter • Oven mitts • Cooling racks • Small saucepan • Wooden spoon • Teaspoon • Tea strainer or small sieve

1 Place the pecans in the food processor or in the blender and close the lid. With an adult's assistance, process until the nuts are finely ground. Unplug the machine and pour the nuts in one of the small mixing bowls.

2 Pour the cracker crumbs into the second small bowl.

3 Place the flour, baking powder, and cinnamon in the third small bowl and stir them together with your fingers.

4 Put the butter and sugar in the mixer bowl. Using the electric mixer, beat until the mixture looks pale yellow and creamy. Break the egg into the batter and add the vanilla; mix until smooth. Add the ground nuts and cracker crumbs and mix until blended.

5 Add the flour mixture ½ cup at a time and mix on low speed until blended after each addition. Scrape the sides of the bowl clean with the rubber spatula and cover the bowl with a piece of plastic wrap. Refrigerate for 1 hour.

6 Place an oven rack in the center of the oven. Then turn on the oven and preheat to 350°F.

7 Sprinkle a little flour on a clean kitchen surface. Break the dough in half and place 1 half on the flour. Press the dough lightly with your hands, then sprinkle a little more flour over the top. Using the rolling pin, roll out the dough ¼ inch thick (see page 11).

8 Press the heart-shaped cookie cutter onto the dough, making sure it cuts right through. Repeat this on the rest of the dough, making as many cookies as you can and leaving a little space between the cookies. Carefully lift up the extra dough so that it separates neatly from the cut cookie shapes. Gather up the extra dough so that it can be rerolled.

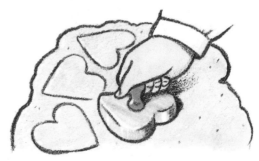

9 Slide a spatula underneath the cookies and place them on a cookie sheet.

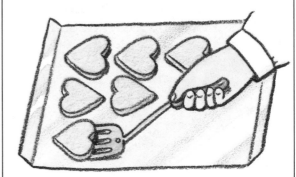

10 Roll out the remaining dough the same way and cut it out. Gather all the extra dough and roll and cut it too. Put all the hearts on cookie sheets and count how many you have. Press the round cutter through the middle of half the heart shapes. Remove the circles from each of the hearts by pinching and lifting them out. Press them together and make 1 extra-large cookie.

11 Put the oven mitts on and put the cookie sheet with the full hearts in the oven. Bake until the cookies turn light golden, about 10 minutes.

12 Wearing the mitts, transfer the cookie sheet to a cooling rack and let them cool while you bake the sheet that has the hearts with the holes in them, about 8 minutes.

13 While the cookies are cooling, place the jam and the water in the saucepan. Put it on the stove and turn the heat to medium-low. Put an oven mitt on for holding the pot handle and gently stir until the jam and water are completely blended.

14 Put each heart cookie with a hole on top of a cookie without a hole. Put a spoonful of jam inside each hole. As the jam cools, it will hold the cookies together.

Easter Daffodil Cake

Preparation time: 30 minutes
Baking time: 45 minutes
Makes: 12 servings

This cake will make a festive centerpiece for any spring party. If you don't have daffodils to put in the center, use daisies or another spring flower.

1 Place an oven rack in the center of the oven. Then turn on the oven and preheat to 350°F.

2 Using the paper towel, spread the 2 teaspoons of butter evenly over the bottom and sides (including the tube) of the cake pan.

INGREDIENTS

¾ cup (1½ sticks) butter, plus 2 teaspoons for the pan, at room temperature
2½ cups all-purpose flour
1 tablespoon baking powder
½ teaspoon ground allspice
½ cup sugar
4 large eggs
1 teaspoon vanilla extract
¾ cup orange juice
1 bunch daffodils, stems cut to 4 inches

UTENSILS

Paper towel • 12-cup tube or Bundt cake pan • Measuring cups and spoons • Medium-size mixing bowl • Mixer bowl • Electric mixer • Rubber spatula • Oven mitts • Cooling rack • Serving plate • Aluminum foil

3 Mix the flour, baking powder, and allspice in the mixing bowl with your fingers or a fork.

4 Put ¾ cup butter and the sugar in the mixer bowl. Using the electric mixer, beat on high speed until pale yellow and creamy.

5 Break the eggs into the butter mixture and beat until they are completely blended. Mix in the vanilla. Scrape the sides of the bowl clean with the rubber spatula.

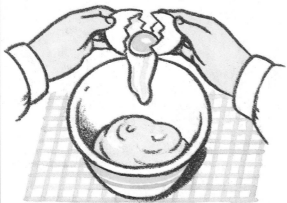

6 Add half the flour mixture and mix on low speed until blended. Add half the orange juice and mix again until blended.

Add the rest of the flour mixture, mix until blended, then blend in the remaining orange juice. The batter should be nice and smooth.

7 Using the rubber spatula, scrape the batter into the prepared pan and spread it evenly.

8 Put the oven mitts on and put the pan in the oven. Bake until the cake pulls away from the side of the pan, about 45 minutes.

9 Wearing the mitts, carefully transfer the pan to the cooling rack. Turn the serving plate upside down over the cake pan. With an adult's assistance, turn the cake over onto the plate and pull the pan up straight off the cake. Let it cool for 10 to 15 minutes.

10 Wrap the daffodil stems in a small piece of aluminum foil and place the flowers in the center of the cake.

Baked Alaska

Preparation time: 30 minutes
Baking time: 3 minutes
Makes: 8 servings

This is a spectacular dessert to serve on a spectacular holiday like the fourth of July.

INGREDIENTS

1 pint vanilla frozen yogurt

1 pint strawberry frozen yogurt

1 prepared pound cake

3 large egg whites, room temperature

¾ cup confectioner's sugar, plus 2 teaspoons to sprinkle over the meringue

UTENSILS

Cutting board • Knife • Ruler • Large mixing bowl • Wooden spoon • Plastic wrap • Mixer bowl • Electric mixer • Measuring cups and spoons • Ovenproof platter • Rubber spatula

1 Remove the frozen yogurt from the freezer to soften slightly.

2 Put the cake on the cutting board and cut into ½-inch slices. Check with the ruler if you are unsure.

Line the inside of the mixing bowl with the slices, cutting some of the slices to fill in the gaps.

3 Scoop the vanilla frozen yogurt into the bowl and spread it smooth with the wooden spoon. Scoop the strawberry frozen yogurt over the vanilla and spread it smooth.

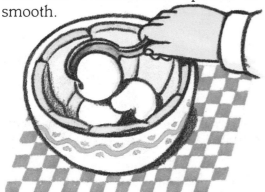

4 Arrange the remaining cake slices over the frozen yogurt. Cover the bowl with plastic wrap and freeze at least 1 hour.

5 About 15 minutes before serving, place an oven rack in the center of the oven. Then turn on the oven and preheat to 450°F.

6 Just before serving, put the egg whites in the mixer bowl. Using the electric mixer, beat on medium speed until the whites are frothy. Increase the speed to high and add 1¼ cups confectioner's sugar 1 tablespoon at a time. Continue to beat until shiny and very stiff. When the beaters are lifted, the peak should not fall.

7 Remove the bowl from the freezer and take off the plastic. Turn the bowl upside down on the platter and let the mold fall out. Using the spatula, spread the egg whites in a thick layer over the mold. Sprinkle with the remaining 2 teaspoons confectioner's sugar.

8 Put the oven mitts on and put the platter in the oven. Bake until the meringue turns golden, about 3 minutes.

9 Wearing the mitts, carefully remove the platter from the oven and serve the baked alaska immediately.

Indian Pudding Pie

Preparation time: 15 minutes
Baking time: 50 to 60 minutes
Makes: 9-inch pie

This pumpkin pie is baked with just a touch of cornmeal to make it more like an Indian pudding and not so different from what the Indians and Pilgrims might have had at their Thanksgiving.

INGREDIENTS

1 can (16 ounces) unsweetened pumpkin puree

¼ cup sugar

2 tablespoons cornmeal

1 tablespoon pumpkin pie spice

2 large eggs

1 cup milk

1 store-bought 9-inch pie shell, unbaked

UTENSILS

Can opener • Wooden spoon • Medium-size mixing bowl • Measuring cups and spoons • Whisk • Baking sheet • Oven mitts • Cooling rack

1 Place one of the oven racks in the center of the oven. Then turn on the oven and preheat to 350°F.

2 Open the can of pumpkin with the can opener and spoon it into the mixing bowl. Add the sugar, cornmeal, and pie spice and whisk until blended.

3 Break the eggs into the bowl and whisk until smooth. Pour in the milk and whisk until blended.

4 Put the pie shell in its pan on the baking sheet. Pour the pumpkin mixture into the shell.

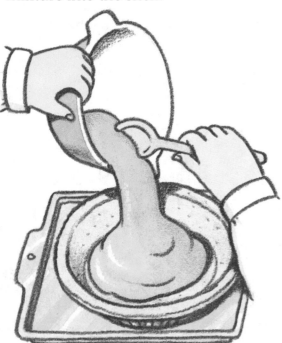

5 Put the oven mitts on and put the baking sheet in the oven. Bake about 50 minutes. To test the pie for doneness, put the oven mitts on, pull the rack out a little, and carefully stick a toothpick into the center. If it comes out clean, then the pie is ready. If not, let the pie bake another 10 minutes.

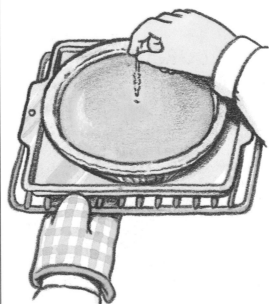

6 Wearing the mitts, carefully transfer the baking sheet to the cooling rack. Let the pie cool at least 20 minutes before serving.

Noodle Pudding

Preparation time: 30 minutes
Baking time: 1 hour
Makes: 12 servings

It doesn't have to be Hanukkah for your family to enjoy this traditional noodle pudding.

INGREDIENTS

1 package (12 ounces) egg noodles

½ cup (1 stick) butter, plus 2 teaspoons for the pan

1 cup sour cream

1 cup ricotta cheese

¼ cup sugar

½ teaspoon ground cinnamon

6 large eggs

UTENSILS

Large saucepan • Wooden spoon • Paper towel • 13 x 9-inch baking pan • Colander or sieve • Oven mitts • Large mixing bowl • Measuring cups and spoons • Knife • Metal spatula

1 Fill the saucepan half full with cold water. Heat over high heat until the water boils. Pour in the noodles and stir with the wooden spoon. Boil the noodles uncovered for 10 minutes.

2 Meanwhile, place an oven rack in the center of the oven. Then turn on the oven and preheat to 350°F. Using the paper towel, spread the 2 teaspoons of butter evenly over the bottom and sides of the baking pan.

3 When the noodles are cooked, put the colander in the sink. Put on the oven mitts, and with an adult's assistance, pour the noodles into the colander. (There will be a lot of steam, so don't lean your face over the sink.)

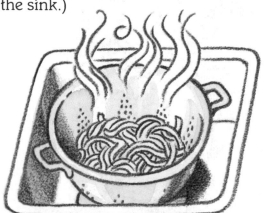

Let the noodles drain for about 1 minute, then shake the colander to get rid of any more water. Pour the hot noodles into the mixing bowl.

4 Break the ½ cup of butter into smaller pieces with your hands and add them to the noodles. Stir the noodles with the wooden spoon until the butter is melted.

5 Add the sour cream, ricotta, sugar, and cinnamon. Stir until the noodles are evenly coated and the sugar and cinnamon are all mixed in.

6 Break the eggs into the noodles and stir until they are completely blended.

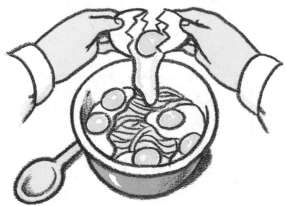

7 Pour the noodle mixture into the prepared baking pan.

8 Put the oven mitts on and put the pan in the oven. Bake for 1 hour. With your oven mitts on, test the pudding for doneness. Pull out the oven rack enough to insert a knife into the center of the pudding. If the blade is clean when you pull it out, the pudding is done. If the knife has custard on it, let the pudding bake another 10 minutes.

9 Wearing the mitts, carefully transfer the pan to a heatproof surface.

10 Using the knife, cut the pudding into 3 strips lengthwise and 4 strips crosswise. Slide the metal spatula under each square and lift it onto a plate. Serve warm.

Sugar Plum Cake

Preparation time: 30 minutes
Baking time: 50 minutes
Makes: 8-inch cake

This is a quick Christmas cake that has glacé fruit dotted throughout. Glacé fruits are fruits that are preserved in a sugar syrup and then sometimes colored. They will begin showing up in your grocery store right about the time you start feeling the first twinges of the holiday spirit.

INGREDIENTS

¾ cup (1½ sticks) butter, plus
  2 teaspoons for the pan,
  at room temperature
1½ cups all-purpose flour
1 teaspoon baking powder
½ teaspoon ground cinnamon
¼ teaspoon ground nutmeg
¾ cup sugar
3 large eggs
1 cup raisins
½ cup shredded unsweetened coconut
1 cup coarsely chopped walnuts
1 cup glacé fruits (with cherries)

UTENSILS

Paper towel • 8-inch cake pan •
Measuring cups and spoons • Small
mixing bowl • Mixer bowl • Electric
mixer • Rubber spatula • Oven mitts •
Cooling rack

1 Place an oven rack in the center of the oven. Then turn on the oven and preheat to 350°F.

2 Using the paper towel, spread the 2 teaspoons of butter evenly over the bottom and sides of the cake pan.

3 Mix the flour, baking powder, cinnamon, and nutmeg in the small mixing bowl with your fingers or a fork.

4 Put ¾ cup butter and the sugar in the mixer bowl. Using the electric mixer, beat on high speed until pale yellow and creamy. Stop every once in a while to scrape the sides of the bowl clean with the rubber spatula.

5 Break the eggs into the butter mixture and beat until they are completely blended.

6 Add the flour mixture and mix on low speed until smooth.

7 Add the raisins, coconut, walnuts, and glacé fruits. Mix on the lowest speed until they are evenly distributed through the batter.

8 Using the rubber spatula, scrape the batter into the prepared pan and spread it evenly.

9 Put the oven mitts on and put the pan in the oven. Bake until the cake has pulled away from the side of the pan, 40 to 50 minutes.

10 Wearing the mitts, carefully transfer the pan to the cooling rack. Let it cool for 10 minutes. Then put the mitts back on and turn the pan upside down onto the rack, letting the cake fall out.

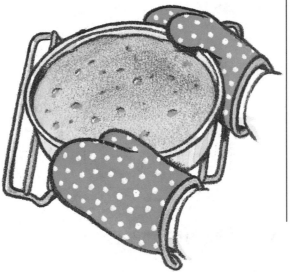

Take the mitts off and carefully turn the cake right side up. Let the cake cool completely before serving.

For U Santa. Love, B.

SWEET TARTS AND COOKIES

ORANGE JUICE TART • SPRING STRAWBERRY BASKETS • TEENY TINY PEANUT SHORTBREAD • NUTTY NESTS • MOON COOKIES • SAND DOLLARS • LITTLE BROWN SPICE COOKIES • THUMBPRINT CLUES • VANILLA WAFERS SNICKERDOODLES • RUSSIAN TEA CAKES WARM GINGERBREAD • POSTMAN'S ENVELOPES • CHEWY RAISIN SQUARES

Orange Juice Tart

Preparation time: 60 minutes
Baking time: 30 minutes
Makes: 9-inch tart

This is a very sophisticated dessert that will brighten up any table. If you don't have time to make the tart shell, you can buy one already made at the grocery store and prepare just the filling yourself. The filling is also good spooned onto Thumbprint Clues made with an extra big print (bake the cookies on page 84 and then fill them). This tart can be served with Unsweetened Whipped Cream (see page 11).

INGREDIENTS

DOUGH:

¾ cup (1½ sticks) butter, at room temperature

¼ cup sugar

1 large egg

½ teaspoon vanilla extract

1½ cups all-purpose flour, plus ¼ cup for rolling out the dough

FILLING:

¼ cup cornstarch

3 cups orange juice

4 large egg yolks (see page 10 for separating eggs)

½ cup frozen orange juice concentrate, thawed

¼ cup sugar

2 tablespoons butter, cold

UTENSILS

Measuring cups and spoons • Mixer bowl • Electric mixer • 9-inch tart pan • Aluminum foil • Baking sheet • Oven mitts • Cooling rack • Small mixing bowl • Whisk • Heavy medium saucepan • Wooden spoon

1 Place an oven rack in the center of the oven. Then turn on the oven and preheat to 350°F.

2 Make the dough: Place the butter and sugar in the mixer bowl. Using the electric mixer, beat until the mixture is completely blended and creamy.

3 Break the egg into the bowl and add the vanilla. Beat on medium speed until blended.

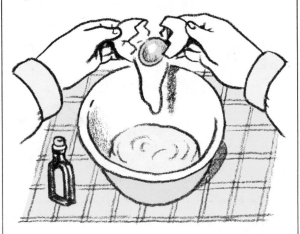

4 Add 1½ cups flour and beat until smooth, about 1 minute.

5 Sprinkle ¼ cup flour on a clean kitchen surface. Put the dough on the floured surface and press it together with your hands until smooth. Put the dough in the tart pan and press it evenly over the bottom and up the sides of the pan.

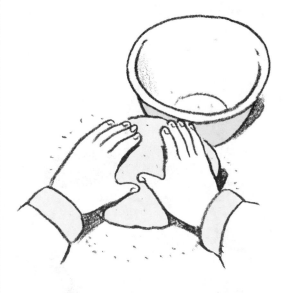

6 Line the tart shell with a piece of aluminum foil. Put the pan on the baking sheet.

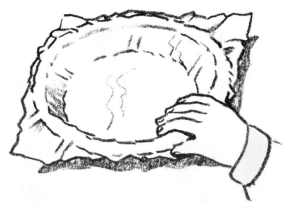

7 Put the oven mitts on and put the baking sheet in the oven. Bake until the edge of the shell is golden brown, about 35 minutes.

8 Wearing the mitts, transfer the baking sheet to the cooling rack. Remove the aluminum foil and let the tart shell cool.

9 Meanwhile, make the filling: Put the cornstarch and ½ cup orange juice in the mixing bowl and whisk them together until the cornstarch is completely dissolved.

Add the egg yolks and whisk until completely blended.

10 Put the remaining 2½ cups orange juice, the orange juice concentrate, and the sugar in the saucepan. Heat over medium-high heat, stirring with the wooden spoon (put on an oven mitt for holding the pot handle), until it starts to boil. With an adult's assistance, pour the egg yolk mixture into the juice while whisking quickly.

Continue to whisk until the mixture returns to boiling. Turn the heat off and add the butter. Whisk constantly until it disappears.

11 Carefully pour the orange cream into the tart shell. Let it cool for 30 minutes before serving.

Spring Strawberry Baskets

Preparation time: 45 minutes   Baking time: 25 minutes
Makes: 10 baskets

INGREDIENTS

DOUGH:

1 cup (2 sticks) butter, plus 1 tablespoon for the pan, at room temperature

½ cup sugar

1 large egg

½ teaspoon vanilla extract

3 cups all-purpose flour, plus ¼ cup for rolling out the dough

FILLING:

2 pints strawberries

6 fresh mint leaves or ¼ teaspoon dried mint

Plain yogurt

UTENSILS

Paper towel • Measuring cups and spoons • 12-cup muffin tin • Mixer bowl • Electric mixer • Rolling pin • Ruler • 5-inch cookie cutter or bowl with a 5-inch diameter • Aluminum foil • Kitchen scissors • Oven mitts • Cooling rack • Cutting board • Knife • Large mixing bowl • Wooden spoon

You know that winter is gone for good once fresh strawberries start showing up in the market. Celebrate by making these baskets to fill with the bright red springtime fruit.

1 Place an oven rack in the center of the oven. Then turn on the oven and preheat to 350°F. Using the paper towel, lightly coat 10 muffin cups with the 1 tablespoon of butter.

2 Make the dough: Place 1 cup butter and the sugar in the mixer bowl. Using the electric mixer, beat until the mixture looks creamy and pale yellow.

Break the egg into the butter mixture and add the vanilla. Mix until blended.

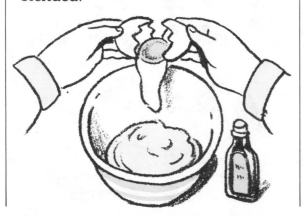

3 Add 3 cups flour 1 cup at a time and mix on low speed until blended after each addition. If the dough becomes too stiff for the mixer, you can mix it together with a spoon or your hands.

4 Sprinkle a little flour on a clean kitchen surface. Break the dough in half and place 1 half on the floured surface. Set the other half aside. Press the dough lightly with your hands, then sprinkle a little more flour over the top. Using the rolling pin, roll out the dough ¼ inch thick (see page 11).

Using the cookie cutter or bowl, cut out 5-inch circles of dough.

5 Place each circle in a muffin cup and gently press the dough to the sides and bottom to make a smooth basket. Using the scissors, cut off the extra dough on top.

6 Repeat with the other half of the dough. Then line each dough basket with a small square of aluminum foil.

7 Put the oven mitts on and put the muffin tin in the oven. Bake for 20 minutes.

8 Wearing the mitts, remove the tin to a heatproof surface. Take out all the pieces of aluminum foil and return the tin to the oven. Bake until the dough is a light golden brown, about 5 minutes longer.

9 Put the mitts back on and transfer the tin to the cooling rack. Let the baskets cool completely, then lift them out of the tin.

10 While the baskets are cooling, pull the hulls off the berries.

Place the berries on the cutting board and slice them, using the knife.

Using the scissors, cut the mint leaves into thin strips. Combine the berries and mint in the mixing bowl.

11 Just before serving, put a spoonful of yogurt in each basket, then fill the basket with strawberries. Put another small spoonful of yogurt on top.

Did You Know?

The largest strawberry ever grown weighed ½ pound.

Teeny Tiny Peanut Shortbread

Preparation time: 25 minutes
Baking time: 25 minutes
Makes: 9-inch shortbread

These shortbread cookies are made the way the Scots have made them for hundreds of years. But our cookies have a flavor kids love best—peanut butter.

INGREDIENTS

½ cup (1 stick) butter, at room temperature

¼ cup peanut butter

¼ cup sugar

½ cup unsalted peanuts

1½ cups all-purpose flour

UTENSILS

Measuring cups and spoons • Mixer bowl • Electric mixer • Rubber spatula • 9-inch pie plate • Fork • Oven mitts • Cooling rack

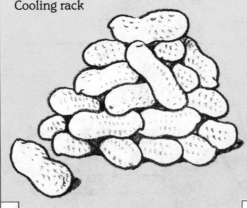

1 Place an oven rack in the center of the oven. Then turn on the oven and preheat to 300°F.

2 Put the butter, peanut butter, and sugar in the mixer bowl. Using the electric mixer, beat on high speed until the mixture is very light and fluffy. Stop every once in a while to scrape the sides of the bowl clean with the rubber spatula.

3 Add the peanuts and mix until evenly distributed through the batter.

4 Add the flour a little at a time and mix until blended. The dough will be crumbly.

5 Use your hands to scoop the dough into the pie plate. Press the dough evenly around the bottom of the pie plate with your fingertips.

Using the fork, prick the dough in straight lines about 1 inch apart.

6 Put the oven mitts on and put the pie plate in the oven. Bake until the dough is very pale brown, 20 to 25 minutes.

7 Wearing the mitts, transfer the pie plate to the cooling rack and let the shortbread cool completely.

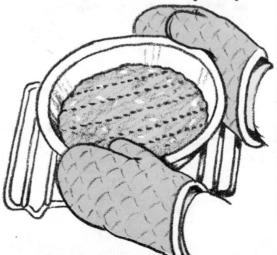

8 Gently ease the shortbread out of the pie plate, then turn it right side up so that you can see the marks from the fork. Break off pieces of shortbread with your fingers. The lines will help break it into straight pieces.

Did You Know?

More than half the peanuts grown every year are made into peanut butter. Guess who eats most of that? Adults!

Nutty Nests

Preparation time: 45 minutes
Total baking time: 1 hour
Makes: 36 cookies

Nutty nests are really meringues—sweet, chewy cookies that go best with a bowl of fresh berries.

INGREDIENTS

¾ cup pecan halves

¼ cup plus 2 tablespoons sugar

¼ teaspoon ground cinnamon

4 large egg whites (see page 10 for separating eggs)

UTENSILS

2 cookie sheets • Waxed paper • Measuring cups and spoons • Food processor or blender • Medium mixing bowl • Fork • Mixer bowl • Electric mixer • Whisk • Teaspoon • Oven mitts • Cooling rack

1 Place an oven rack in the center of the oven. Then turn on the oven and preheat to 250°F. Line each cookie sheet with a piece of waxed paper.

2 Place the pecans in the food processor or half at a time in the blender. With an adult's assistance, process the nuts until finely ground.

Pour the nuts into the mixing bowl. Add ¼ cup sugar and the cinnamon. Stir with the fork until well mixed.

3 Put the egg whites in the mixer bowl. Using the electric mixer,

beat on high speed until the whites are very foamy. With the mixer still on high speed, sprinkle the remaining sugar over the whites 1 tablespoon at a time. When all the sugar has been added, the mixture should be stiff and shiny. If it's not, keep beating.

4 Sprinkle the nut mixture over the meringue and fold them gently together with the whisk.

5 Use the teaspoon to scoop out mounds of the meringue onto the paper-lined baking sheets, pushing each mound off the spoon with your finger. The mounds should be about 1½ inches apart.

6 Put on the oven mitts and put 1 cookie sheet in the oven. Bake until lightly browned, 20 to 30 minutes.

7 Wearing the mitts, transfer the cookie sheet to the cooling rack. Bake the second sheet of meringues. Let the meringues cool completely before peeling them off the waxed paper.

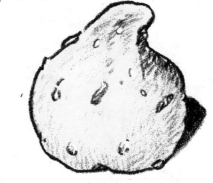

Moon Cookies

Preparation time: 30 minutes
Total baking time: 24 minutes
Makes: 14 full moons

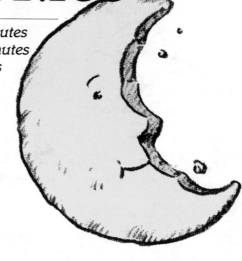

Shape these cookies nice and round, like full moons.

INGREDIENTS

1 cup sliced almonds

¾ cup (1½ sticks) butter, at room temperature

¼ cup sugar

1 large egg

2 teaspoons almond extract

1¼ cups all-purpose flour

½ teaspoon ground nutmeg

UTENSILS

Measuring cups and spoons • Small mixing bowl • Mixer bowl • Electric mixer • Rubber spatula • 2 cookie sheets • Oven mitts • Cooling rack

1 Place an oven rack in the center of the oven. Then turn on the oven and preheat to 350°F.

2 Break the almond slices between your fingers into the mixing bowl, so that the pieces are smaller.

3 Put the butter and sugar in the mixer bowl. Using the electric mixer, beat on medium speed until the mixture is light and fluffy. Stop every once in a while to scrape the sides of the bowl clean with the rubber spatula.

4 Break the egg into the batter and mix at medium-low speed until completely blended. Add the almond extract and mix again until blended.

5 Add half the flour and mix on low speed until smooth. Add the rest of the flour and the nutmeg and mix again.

6 Add the crumbled almonds and mix until they're evenly distributed through the dough.

7 Break off a piece of dough about the size of a golf ball, and, using your hands, roll it into a smooth ball.

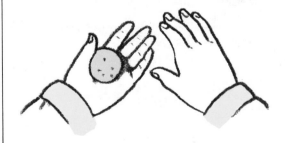

Press the ball into a flat, 2-inch round cookie and put it on a cookie sheet. Make more moons and place them about 1½ inches apart on the cookie sheets.

8 Put the oven mitts on and put a cookie sheet in the oven. Bake until the edges are golden brown, 10 to 12 minutes.

9 Wearing the mitts, transfer the cookie sheet to the cooling rack. Bake the second sheet of cookies. Let the cookies cool completely before eating them.

Sand Dollars

Preparation time: 30 minutes
Refrigeration time: 1 hour
Total baking time: 20 minutes
Makes: 36 cookies

Not all sand dollars are found at the beach. Sometimes, if you're lucky, you can find them in your own kitchen. These sand dollars are baked until they're lightly colored, just like the real thing.

INGREDIENTS

DOUGH:

½ cup (1 stick) butter, at room temperature

½ cup sugar

1 large egg

1 teaspoon almond extract

¼ teaspoon salt

1½ cups all-purpose flour

TOPPING:

1 large egg white (see page 10 for separating eggs)

¼ cup sliced almonds

UTENSILS

Measuring cups and spoons • Mixer bowl • Electric mixer • Rubber spatula • Plastic wrap • Cutting board • Knife • 2 cookie sheets • Oven mitts • Cooling rack

1 Make the dough: Put the butter and sugar in the mixer bowl. Using the electric mixer, beat them on medium speed until the sugar and butter blend together into a soft ball.

2 Break the egg into the batter. Add the almond extract and salt. Mix until blended.

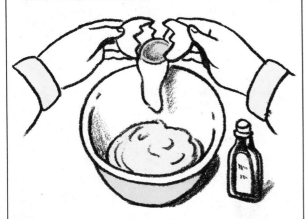

3 With the mixer on medium speed, add the flour a little at a time. When all the flour has been blended, the dough should look crumbly.

FLOUR

4 Turn the dough out onto a clean kitchen surface. Knead the dough until it is smooth and shiny, 3 to 5 minutes (see page 12).

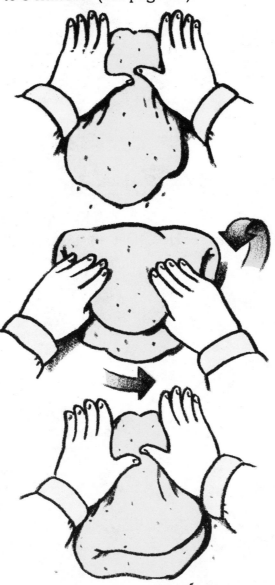

5 Shape the dough into a thick log and wrap it in a piece of plastic wrap. Refrigerate for 1 hour.

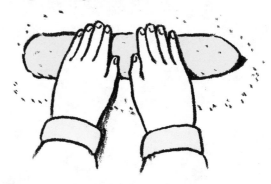

6 Wash and dry the mixer bowl and beaters.

7 After the dough is chilled, place an oven rack in the center of the oven. Then turn on the oven and preheat to 350°F.

8 Unwrap the dough on a cutting board. Using the knife, carefully cut the log into ½-inch-thick slices. Put the slices about 1 inch apart on the cookie sheets.

9 Put the egg white into the mixer bowl. Beat the egg white with the electric mixer until it's very foamy and white. Use your finger to rub egg white over the top of each cookie.

Sprinkle the tops with the almonds.

10 Put the oven mitts on and put a cookie sheet in the oven. Bake until the cookies are golden, about 10 minutes.

11 Wearing the mitts, transfer the cookie sheet to the cooling rack. Bake the second sheet of cookies. Let the cookies cool completely before eating them.

Did You Know?

Almonds are actually "stones" and not nuts. These stones are the ones found in the middle of fruit, like peach stones, and not the ones you pick up from the ground.

Little Brown Spice Cookies

Preparation time: 45 minutes
Total baking time: 10 minutes
Makes: 20 cookies

This crisp spice cookie is great for dunking in hot cocoa or apple cider at a honey bear tea.

INGREDIENTS

1½ cups all-purpose flour, plus ½ cup for kneading and rolling out the dough

½ teaspoon baking soda

1 teaspoon ground cloves

1 teaspoon ground cinnamon

¼ teaspoon ground nutmeg

½ cup (1 stick) butter, plus 2 teaspoons for the cookie sheets, at room temperature

2 tablespoons brown sugar

¼ cup dark corn syrup

1 teaspoon vanilla extract

¾ cup sliced almonds

UTENSILS

Measuring cups and spoons • Large and medium-size mixing bowls • Fork • Mixer bowl • Electric mixer • Rubber spatula • Wooden spoon • Plastic wrap • Paper towel • 2 cookie sheets • Rolling pin • Ruler • 2½-inch round cookie cutter • Oven mitts • Cooling rack • Metal spatula

1 Place 1½ cups flour, the baking soda, cloves, cinnamon, and nutmeg in the medium-size mixing bowl and stir them together with your fingers or the fork.

2 Place ½ cup butter and the brown sugar in the mixer bowl. Using the electric mixer, beat on high speed until the mixture looks light and fluffy.

3 Pour in the corn syrup and beat on medium-high speed until blended. Stop once or twice to scrape the sides of the bowl clean with the rubber spatula.

4 Add the flour mixture and mix on medium speed until smooth. Mix in the vanilla. Then stop the mixer and stir in the almonds, using the wooden spoon or your hands.

5 Sprinkle a clean kitchen surface with a little flour. Place the dough on the floured surface and sprinkle a little more flour on top.

6 Knead the dough (see page 12) until smooth and shiny, 3 to 5 minutes. If necessary, sprinkle more flour over and under it to keep it from sticking to the counter.

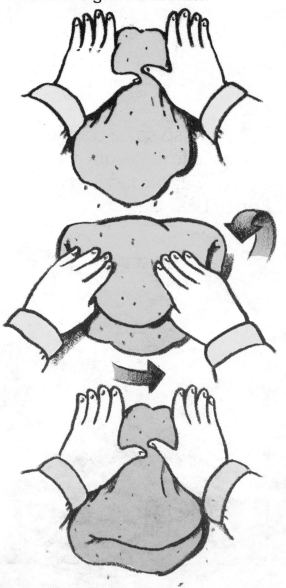

7 Place the dough in the large mixing bowl and cover it with plastic wrap. Refrigerate for 30 minutes.

8 Place an oven rack in the center of the oven. Then turn on the oven and preheat to 400°F. Using the paper towel, rub 1 teaspoon butter over each cookie sheet.

9 Sprinkle a little flour onto a kitchen surface and place the dough on the flour. Roll out the dough ¼ inch thick, using the rolling pin (see page 11). Cut out the dough with the cookie cutter and place the cookies on the buttered sheets, about 1½ inches apart. Stack the scraps and gently press them together. Roll out and cut as many more cookies as you can.

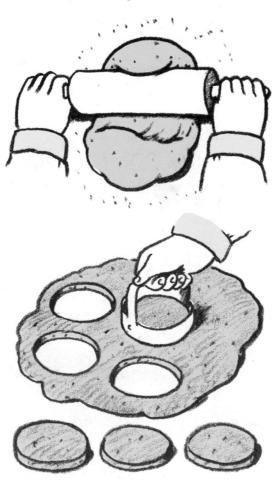

10 Put on the oven mitts and put a cookie sheet in the oven. Bake 5 minutes. The cakes will be crisp around the edges.

11 Wearing the mitts, transfer the cookie sheet to the cooling rack. Bake the second sheet of cookies. Let the cookies cool for a few minutes. Then use the metal spatula to transfer the cookies to the rack to cool completely.

Thumbprint Clues

Preparation time: 25 minutes
Total baking time: 20 minutes
Makes: 40 clues

The clue to each cookie is your thumbprint pressed in the middle and then filled with jam. These clues will disappear fast.

INGREDIENTS

½ cup (1 stick) butter, at room temperature

¼ cup sugar

1 large egg yolk (see page 10 for separating eggs)

½ teaspoon almond extract

1½ cups all-purpose flour

½ cup juice-sweetened strawberry (or your favorite) jam

UTENSILS

Measuring cups and spoons • Mixer bowl • Electric mixer • Rubber spatula • 2 cookie sheets • Oven mitts • Cooling rack

1 Place an oven rack in the center of the oven. Then turn on the oven and preheat to 350°F.

2 Put the butter and sugar in the mixer bowl. Using the electric mixer, beat on medium speed until the mixture is light and fluffy. Stop every once in a while to scrape the sides of the bowl clean with the rubber spatula.

3 Add the egg yolk and almond extract. Mix on medium-high speed until the yolk is completely blended.

4 Add half the flour at a time and mix on low speed after each addition, until smooth and blended.

5 Pinch off a small piece of dough about the size of a quarter. Roll it into a ball between the palms of your hands, then put it on a cookie sheet.

Lightly press your thumb in the ball's center, leaving a cuplike indentation. Shape the rest of the dough in the same way, spacing the cookies about 1 inch apart on the cookie sheets.

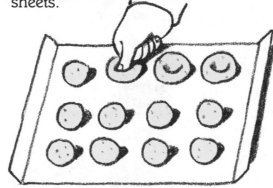

6 Fill each indentation with about ½ teaspoon jam.

7 Put the oven mitts on and put a cookie sheet in the oven. Bake for 10 minutes.

8 Wearing the mitts, transfer the cookie sheet to the cooling rack. Bake the second sheet of cookies. Let the cookies cool completely before eating them.

Vanilla Wafers

Preparation time: 25 minutes
Total baking time: 20 to 24 minutes
Makes: 30 cookies

You'll never know how good vanilla wafers can taste until you make your own. Keep them in an airtight container, so that they'll always taste as good as the day you baked them.

INGREDIENTS

½ cup (1 stick) butter, at room temperature
¼ cup sugar
1 large egg
1½ teaspoons vanilla extract
¾ cup all-purpose flour

UTENSILS

Measuring cups and spoons • Mixer bowl • Electric mixer • Rubber spatula • 2 cookie sheets • Oven mitts • Cooling rack • Metal spatula

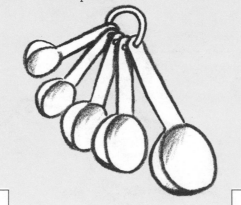

1 Place an oven rack in the center of the oven. Then turn on the oven and preheat to 350°F.

2 Put the butter and sugar in the mixer bowl. Using the electric mixer, beat on medium speed until light and fluffy. Stop every once in a while to scrape the sides of the bowl clean with the rubber spatula.

3 Add the egg and vanilla extract and mix until blended. The dough won't be smooth until the flour is added.

4 With the mixer on low speed, add the flour a spoonful at a time. Keep mixing until the dough is smooth.

5 Using the teaspoon measure, scoop out a spoonful of dough and put it on a cookie sheet. Space the cookies about 1 inch apart. Keep going until all the dough is on the sheets.

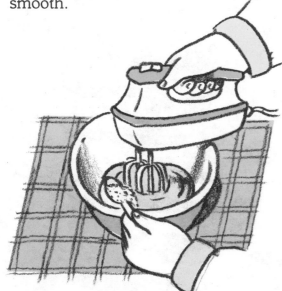

6 Put the oven mitts on and put a cookie sheet in the oven. Bake until the cookies are golden brown around the edges, 10 to 12 minutes.

7 Wearing the mitts, transfer the cookie sheet to the cooling rack. Bake the second sheet of cookies. Let the cookies cool completely before taking them off the sheets with the metal spatula.

Did You Know?

If there isn't a very specialized bee or hummingbird around to pollinate the vanilla vines, each one has to be done by hand.

Snickerdoodles

Preparation time: 25 minutes
Baking time: 10 to 12 minutes
Makes: 30 cookies

These cookies are especially good dipped into a glass of milk. You can make them a little different by adding nuts to the batter along with the raisins.

INGREDIENTS

DOUGH:

1 ¾ cups all-purpose flour

1 teaspoon baking soda

½ teaspoon ground nutmeg

¾ cup (1 ½ sticks) butter, at room temperature

⅓ cup sugar

2 large eggs

2 tablespoons sour cream

¾ cup raisins

TOPPING:

1 teaspoon ground cinnamon

2 teaspoons sugar

UTENSILS

Measuring cups and spoons • Small and medium-size mixing bowls • Mixer bowl • Electric mixer • Rubber spatula • 2 cookie sheets • Oven mitts • Cooling rack

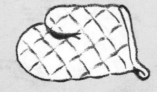

1 Place an oven rack in the center of the oven. Then turn on the oven and preheat to 350°F.

2 Make the dough: Place the flour, baking soda, and nutmeg in the medium mixing bowl and stir them together with your fingers or a fork.

3 Put the butter and sugar in the mixer bowl. Using the electric mixer, beat on medium speed until light and fluffy.

Stop every once in a while and scrape the sides of the bowl clean with the rubber spatula.

4 Break the eggs into the batter and add the sour cream. Mix on medium speed for 1 minute, stopping once or twice to scrape the sides of the bowl clean.

5 Add 1 cup of the flour mixture to the batter. Mix on low speed until blended. Add the rest of the flour mixture and mix again until blended.

6 Add the raisins and mix until they are evenly distributed throughout the dough.

7 Using the tablespoon measure, scoop mounds of dough onto the cookie sheets, placing them about 1 inch apart.

8 Make the topping: Stir the cinnamon and sugar together in the small mixing bowl with your fingers.

Sprinkle a pinch of the cinnamon sugar over each cookie.

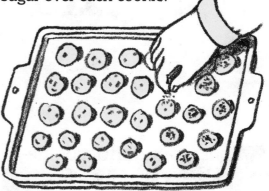

9 Put on the oven mitts and put a cookie sheet in the oven. Bake until the cookies are golden brown around the edges, about 10 minutes.

10 Wearing the mitts, transfer the cookie sheet to the cooling rack. Bake the second sheet of cookies. Let the cookies cool completely on the cookie sheets before eating them. Keep these cookies in an airtight container so they stay fresh.

Russian Tea Cakes

Preparation time: 45 minutes
Total baking time: 30 minutes
Makes: 40 cakes

These wonderful cookie-cakes take only a few minutes to bake, but never look done even when they are. The best way to check is to remove the cookie sheet from the oven (with the oven mitts on), carefully lift up a cookie with a metal spatula, and if the bottom is brown, the cookies are baked.

INGREDIENTS

1½ cups walnut halves

1 cup (2 sticks) butter, at room temperature

½ cup granulated sugar

2½ cups all-purpose flour

1 teaspoon ground cinnamon

½ teaspoon salt

½ cup confectioner's sugar

UTENSILS

Measuring cups and spoons • Food processor or blender • Mixer bowl • Electric mixer • 2 cookie sheets • Oven mitts • Cooling rack • Medium-size mixing bowl

1 Place all the nuts in the food processor or 1 cup at a time in the blender. Place the lid on the machine. With an adult's assistance, process the nuts until finely ground. Set aside.

2 Place an oven rack in the center of the oven. Then turn on the oven and preheat to 350°F.

3 Place the butter and granulated sugar in the mixer bowl. Using the electric mixer, beat on medium-high speed until the mixture looks light and fluffy.

4 Add the flour, a little at a time, and mix on medium speed after each addition until smooth. Add the cinnamon and salt and beat until completely blended. Add the ground nuts and mix thoroughly. The dough will be crumbly but it should hold together when rolled in your hands.

5 Using your hands, shape the dough into small balls ¾ inch wide (the size of a large gumball). Place the cookie balls about 1 inch apart on the cookie sheets.

6 Put on the oven mitts and put a cookie sheet in the oven. Bake for 15 minutes.

7 Wearing the mitts, transfer the cookie sheet to the cooling rack. (The note at the beginning of the recipe explains how to know if the cookies are done.) Bake the second sheet of cookies. Let the cookies cool for about 5 minutes.

8 Put the confectioner's sugar in the mixing bowl. When the cookies are cool enough to touch, roll each one in the sugar and put it on the cooling rack. Repeat with the remaining cookies.

Warm Gingerbread

Preparation time: 20 minutes
Baking time: 30 minutes
Makes: 9-inch square cake

Have a pan of warm gingerbread ready to serve to all the tree trimmers at your house. The aroma of it baking will "deck the halls" while they work, giving a nice touch to the festivities.

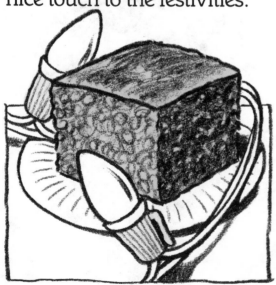

INGREDIENTS

1 cup (2 sticks) butter, plus 2 teaspoons for the pan, at room temperature
3 cups all-purpose flour
1½ teaspoons baking soda
1 tablespoon ground ginger
1 tablespoon ground cinnamon
¼ cup (packed) brown sugar
3 large eggs
½ cup sour cream
⅓ cup molasses

UTENSILS

Paper towel • 9-inch square baking pan • Measuring cups and spoons • Medium-size mixing bowl • Mixer bowl • Electric mixer • Rubber spatula • Oven mitts • Cooling rack • Knife

1 Place an oven rack in the center of the oven. Then turn on the oven and preheat to 350°F.

2 Using the paper towel, rub the 2 teaspoons of butter evenly over the bottom and sides of the baking pan.

3 Place the flour, baking soda, ginger, and cinnamon in the mixing bowl and stir them together with your fingers or a fork.

4 Place the 1 cup of butter and the brown sugar in the mixer bowl. Using the electric mixer, beat on high speed until pale brown and creamy.

5 Break the eggs into the butter mixture and beat until completely blended.

6 Add half the flour mixture and mix on low speed until smooth. Then add the sour cream and mix until blended. Add the remaining flour and mix until blended. Add the molasses and mix the batter until smooth.

7 Using the rubber spatula, scrape the batter into the prepared pan and smooth the top.

8 Put the oven mitts on and put the pan in the oven. Bake until the gingerbread has shrunk away from the sides of the pan, about 30 minutes.

9 Wearing the mitts, transfer the pan to the cooling rack. Let the gingerbread cool slightly. Cut into squares with the knife and serve.

Postman's Envelopes

Preparation time: 40 minutes
Refrigeration time: 30 minutes
Total baking time: 30 minutes
Makes: 30 cookies

Here are some really tiny surprise-filled cookie packages. Remember to let them cool completely before eating them—the filling will not cool down as fast as the dough.

INGREDIENTS

DOUGH:

½ cup (1 stick) butter, at room temperature

¼ pound cream cheese, at room temperature

2 tablespoons sugar

1 cup all-purpose flour, plus ¼ cup for rolling out the dough

FILLING:

¾ cup pecan halves or chopped pecans

½ cup juice-sweetened raspberry (or your favorite) jam

UTENSILS

Measuring cups and spoons • Mixer bowl • Electric mixer • Plastic wrap • Small mixing bowl • Spoon • Rolling pin • Ruler • Knife • 2 cookie sheets

1 Make the dough: Put the butter and cream cheese in the mixer bowl. Using the electric mixer, beat on medium speed until smooth and blended.

2 Add the sugar and beat until mixed in. Add ½ cup flour and beat on medium speed until blended. Add the remaining ½ cup flour and beat again until blended.

3 Cover the bowl with plastic wrap and refrigerate for 30 minutes.

4 While the dough is chilling, make the filling: Break the pecan halves, if you're using them, into small pieces with your fingers.

Stir the pecans and jam together in the small mixing bowl. Set aside until you're ready to fill the dough packages.

5 After the dough is chilled, place an oven rack in the center of the oven. Then turn on the oven and preheat to 350°F.

6 Sprinkle a little flour on a clean kitchen surface. Take the dough out of the bowl and put it on the floured surface. Press the dough lightly with your hands to even it out.

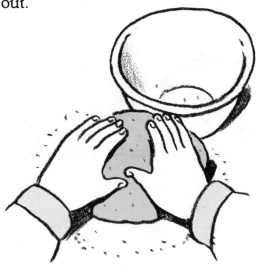

Sprinkle a little more flour over the top. Using the rolling pin, roll out the dough ⅛ inch thick (see page 11).

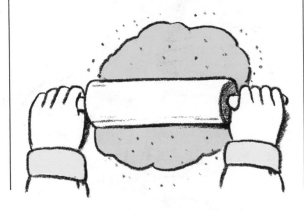

7 Using the edge of the ruler and the knife, cut one edge of the dough straight. Measure 2 inches from the first cut and make another cut in a straight line. Keep cutting straight lines 2 inches apart until you reach the other edge of the dough.

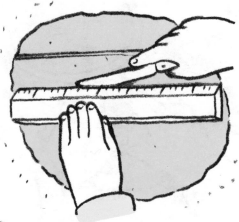

8 Now place the ruler across the straight lines and cut more lines 2 inches apart, so that the dough is cut into 2-inch squares.

9 Spoon ½ teaspoon filling on the center of each square.

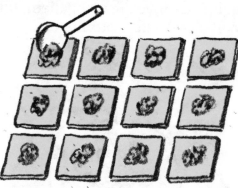

Fold each square in half to make a triangle, then press the edges tightly together with your fingertips. Put the filled packages on the cookie sheets.

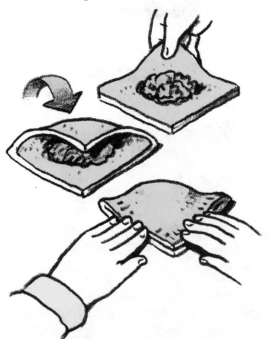

10 Put the oven mitts on and put a cookie sheet in the oven. Bake until the cookies are golden brown around the edges, about 15 minutes.

11 Wearing the mitts, transfer the cookie sheet to the cooling rack. Bake the second sheet of cookies. Let the cookies cool completely before eating them.

Chewy Raisin Squares

Preparation time: 30 minutes
Baking time: 25 minutes
Makes: 24 squares

They look like brownies, but are much lighter. What makes the mocha flavor is a combination of chocolate and coffee.

INGREDIENTS

¾ cup (1½ sticks) butter, plus 2 teaspoons for the pan, at room temperature

1 cup all-purpose flour

2 tablespoons unsweetened cocoa powder

2 teaspoons decaffeinated instant coffee

1½ teaspoons baking powder

½ cup sugar

2 large eggs

1 teaspoon vanilla extract

½ cup raisins

1 cup coarsely chopped walnuts

UTENSILS

Paper towel • 13 x 9-inch baking pan • Measuring cups and spoons • Small mixing bowl • Mixer bowl • Electric mixer • Rubber spatula • Oven mitts • Cooling rack • Knife

1 Place an oven rack in the center of the oven. Then turn on the oven and preheat to 350°F.

2 Using the paper towel, spread the 2 teaspoons of butter evenly over the bottom and sides of the baking pan.

3 Mix the flour, cocoa, instant coffee, and baking powder in the small mixing bowl with your fingers or a fork.

4 Put the ¾ cup of butter and the sugar in the mixer bowl. Using the electric mixer, beat on high speed until pale yellow and creamy.

5 Break the eggs into the butter mixture and beat until they are completely blended. Add the vanilla and beat again until blended.

6 Add the flour mixture and mix on low speed until the batter is smooth.

7 Add the raisins and walnuts and mix until they are evenly distributed through the batter.

8 Using the rubber spatula, scrape the batter into the prepared pan and spread it evenly.

9 Put the oven mitts on and put the pan in the oven. Bake until the cake pulls away slightly from the sides of the pan, 25 minutes.

10 Wearing the mitts, carefully transfer the pan to the cooling rack. Let cool for at least 15 minutes. Using the knife, cut the cake into 2-inch squares.

SIDE BAKES

DILLY BREAD • POPOVERS • SOFT PRETZELS

Dilly Bread

Preparation time: 45 minutes
Rising time: 1½ hours
Baking time: 50 minutes
Makes: 1 round loaf

When there's a roast for dinner, make this bread to go along with it. It's a cinch to prepare because it doesn't have to be kneaded very much.

INGREDIENTS

¼ cup warm water

1 package (about 1 tablespoon) active dry yeast

1 cup small curd cottage cheese

2 tablespoons sugar

2 tablespoons dried onion flakes

4 teaspoons dried dill

1 teaspoon salt

1 teaspoon baking soda

2 tablespoons plus 2 teaspoons vegetable oil

1 large egg

2½ cups all-purpose flour, plus additional if needed for kneading the dough

UTENSILS

Large mixing bowl • Measuring cups and spoons • Wooden spoon • Paper towel • Kitchen towel • 1½-quart round casserole • Oven mitts • Cooling rack

1 Pour the water into the mixing bowl. Sprinkle on the yeast and stir with the wooden spoon until the yeast is dissolved in the water.

2 Add the cottage cheese, sugar, onion flakes, dill, salt, baking soda, and 1 tablespoon oil. Stir until blended. Break the egg into the bowl and stir again until blended.

3 Add 2½ cups flour and stir until the dough is too stiff to stir anymore. Then scoop the dough out

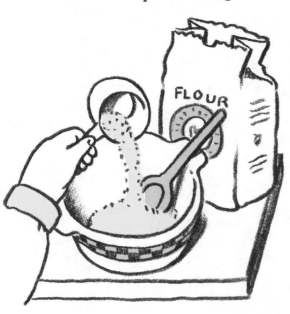

onto a clean kitchen surface and knead until smooth (see page 12). Add a little more flour if the dough starts to stick.

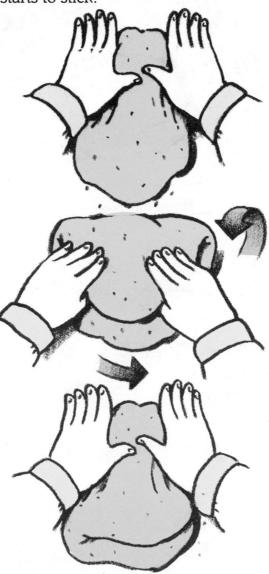

4 Wash and dry the mixing bowl. Pour the 2 teaspoons of oil into the bowl and spread it over the bottom and sides with the paper towel. Put the dough in the bowl, then turn it over so that the top is oiled. Cover the bowl with the kitchen towel and put the bowl in a warm place that isn't drafty. Let it rise until the dough has doubled in size, about 1 hour.

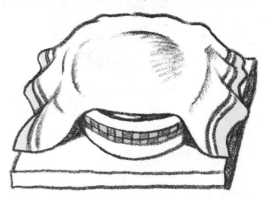

5 Pour 1 tablespoon oil into the casserole and spread it over the bottom and sides with the paper towel.

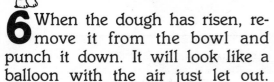

6 When the dough has risen, remove it from the bowl and punch it down. It will look like a balloon with the air just let out.

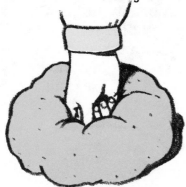

Shape the dough into a ball and put it in the oiled casserole. Cover it with the kitchen towel and let it rise until the dough is as high as the top of the casserole, about 30 minutes.

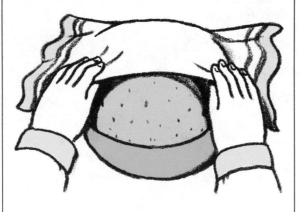

7 Place an oven rack in the center of the oven. Then turn on the oven and preheat to 350°F.

8 When the dough has risen again, put on the oven mitts and put the casserole in the oven. Bake for 50 minutes.

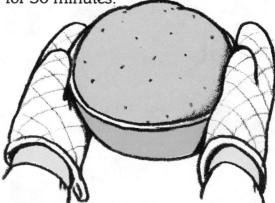

9 Wearing the mitts, transfer the casserole to a heatproof surface. Turn the casserole upside down and let the bread fall out. Put the bread on the cooling rack to cool.

Popovers

Preparation time: 15 minutes
Baking time: 35 minutes
Makes: 12 popovers

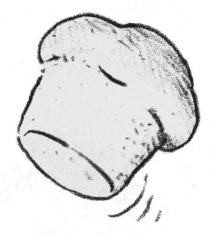

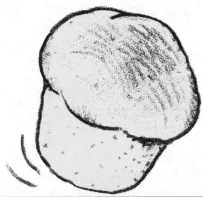

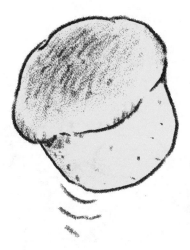

It's magic—the batter goes in flat and bakes up puffed and golden!

INGREDIENTS

2 teaspoons solid vegetable shortening for the tin
2 large eggs
1 cup milk
1 tablespoon vegetable oil
1 cup all-purpose flour
1 teaspoon salt

UTENSILS

Paper towel • Measuring cups and spoons • 12-cup muffin tin • Mixer bowl • Electric mixer • Rubber spatula • Oven mitts • Cooling rack • Fork

1 Place an oven rack in the center of the oven. Then turn on the oven and preheat to 400°F.

2 Using the paper towel, spread the shortening evenly over the bottoms and sides of the muffin cups.

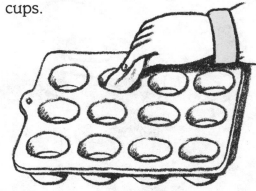

3 Break the eggs into the mixer bowl. Add the milk and oil. Using the electric mixer, mix on low speed until blended.

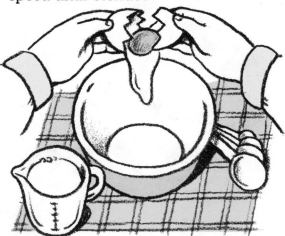

4 Add the flour and salt and mix on medium speed for 2 minutes. The batter should be smooth. Stop at least once to scrape the sides of the bowl clean with the rubber spatula.

5 Using the ¼-cup measure, scoop batter into each muffin cup. The cups should be filled about halfway.

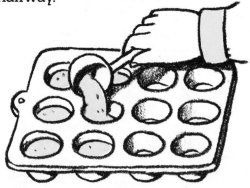

6 Put the oven mitts on and put the tin in the oven. Bake until the popovers are puffed and golden brown, about 35 minutes.

7 Wearing the mitts, carefully transfer the tin to the cooling rack. Tilt the pan to let the popovers fall out. Remove any stubborn popovers with a fork. Serve them while they're hot with butter and jam.

Soft Pretzels

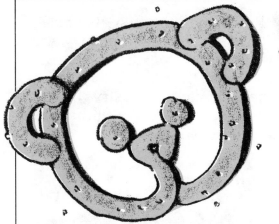

Preparation time: 40 minutes
Total baking time: 30 to 40 minutes
Makes: 12 pretzels

Shape the pretzel dough in letters that spell out your name or the names of your best friends.

1 Place an oven rack in the center of the oven. Then turn on the oven and preheat to 425°F.

2 Using the paper towel, spread the shortening evenly over both cookie sheets.

INGREDIENTS

1 tablespoon vegetable shortening for the baking sheets

1⅓ cups warm water

1 package (about 1 tablespoon) active dry yeast

1 tablespoon sugar

½ teaspoon table salt

3¼ cups all-purpose flour

1 large egg

1 tablespoon water

2 tablespoons coarse salt

UTENSILS

Paper towel • 2 cookie sheets • Measuring cups and spoons • Large mixing bowl • Wooden spoon • Ruler • Small bowl • Small whisk or fork • Pastry brush • Oven mitts • Metal spatula • Cooling rack

3 Pour the warm water into the mixing bowl. Sprinkle the yeast over the water and let it stand about 5 minutes to soften. Then stir with the wooden spoon until completely blended.

4 Add the sugar, table salt, and 1 cup flour; stir until blended. Add 2 more cups of flour ½ cup at a time, stirring to blend after each addition. The dough should be well blended.

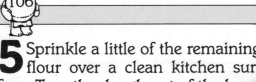

5 Sprinkle a little of the remaining flour over a clean kitchen surface. Turn the dough out of the bowl onto the floured surface. Knead

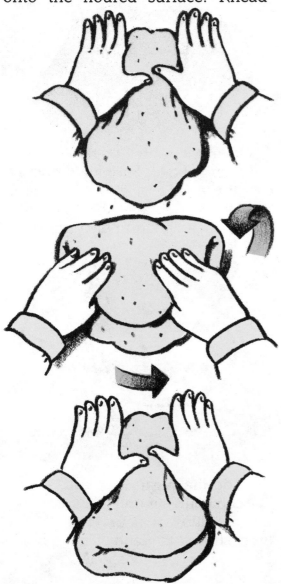

(page 12) until the dough is smooth and elastic, sprinkling with flour if the dough is sticky.

6 Pull the dough into 12 equal pieces. Roll 1 piece into a rope about 15 inches long, then shape the rope into a pretzel or letter.

Put the pretzel on one of the baking sheets and repeat with the remaining pieces of dough.

7 Break the egg into the small bowl. Add 1 tablespoon water and stir them together with the whisk. Brush the egg wash over each pretzel, using the pastry brush. Sprinkle the coarse salt over the pretzels with your fingers.

8 Put the oven mitts on and put a baking sheet in the oven. Bake until the pretzels are golden brown, 15 to 20 minutes.

9 Wearing the mitts, carefully transfer the sheet to a heatproof surface. Bake the second sheet of pretzels. Using the spatula, transfer the pretzels from the baked sheet to the rack to cool a little before serving them. Cool the remaining pretzels when they are finished baking.

BIG DEALS

CHOCOLATE DREAM CAKE • APPLE ALMOND TEA CAKE • CUSTARD CUPS • PUFFED EXPLOSIONS • "THE BIG CHEESE" CAKE • APPLE CHARLOTTE • AUSTRIAN SOUFFLE WASHINGTON'S CHERRY TREE • FALL HARVEST APPLE AND CHEDDAR PIE

Chocolate Dream Cake

Preparation time: 30 minutes
Baking time: 35 minutes
Makes: 9-inch cake

This unusual chocolate cake—it uses graham crackers instead of flour— bakes up light but with a rich flavor. The best!

INGREDIENTS

1 teaspoon butter for the pan
2 tablespoons all-purpose flour for the pan
1 cup semisweet chocolate chips
1 cup walnuts or pecans
½ cup graham cracker crumbs (6 whole crackers; see Tip)
¼ teaspoon ground cinnamon
¼ teaspoon ground cloves
5 large eggs, at room temperature
¼ cup sugar
Unsweetened Whipped Cream for serving, optional (see page 11)

UTENSILS

Paper towel • 9-inch cake pan • Measuring cups and spoons • Blender or food processor • 2 small and 1 large mixing bowls • Mixer bowl • Electric mixer • Rubber spatula • Oven mitts • Cooling rack • Serving plate • Knife

1 Using the paper towel, spread the butter evenly over the bottom and sides of the cake pan. Add the flour to the pan; slowly turn and shake the pan to coat the inside with flour. Turn the pan upside down over the sink and shake out the excess flour.

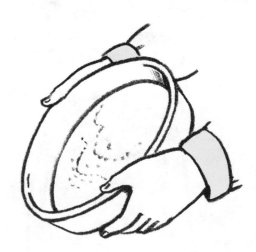

2 Place an oven rack in the center of the oven. Then turn on the oven and preheat to 375°F.

3 Put the chocolate chips and nuts in the blender or food processor fitted with the steel blade. With an adult's assistance, put the cover on the machine and process a few seconds to chop the chips and nuts.

4 Put the cracker crumbs, cinnamon, and cloves in a small mixing bowl and stir them together with your fingers or a fork.

5 Separate the eggs (see page 10), placing the yolks in the mixer bowl and the whites in the second small bowl.

6 Add the sugar to the egg yolks. Using the electric mixer, beat on high speed until pale yellow and creamy. Add the chocolate mixture and mix on low speed until blended. Add the cracker crumb mixture and mix again until blended. Stop every once in a while to scrape the sides of the bowl clean with the spatula.

Scrape the egg yolk mixture into the large mixing bowl.

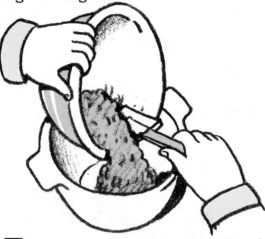

7 Wash and dry the mixer bowl and beater. Pour the egg whites into the mixer bowl. Using the electric mixer, beat on high speed until very white and fluffy. When the beater is lifted, the peak should stand without falling.

8 Using the rubber spatula, scrape the egg whites over the egg yolk mixture.

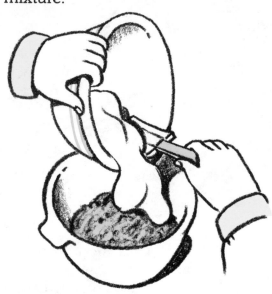

Fold in the egg whites by gently moving the spatula through the mixture from the bottom of the bowl to the top and then down again. Keep folding until all the egg whites have disappeared into the batter.

9 Scrape the batter into the pan and spread evenly.

10 Put the oven mitts on and put the pan in the oven. Bake until the cake has pulled away slightly from the sides of the pan, 30 to 35 minutes.

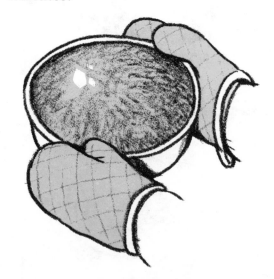

11 Wearing the mitts, carefully transfer the pan to a heatproof surface. Put the cooling rack on top of the cake and turn the rack and the pan over, letting the cake fall onto the rack. Pull the pan up straight off the cake and let it cool for about 15 minutes.

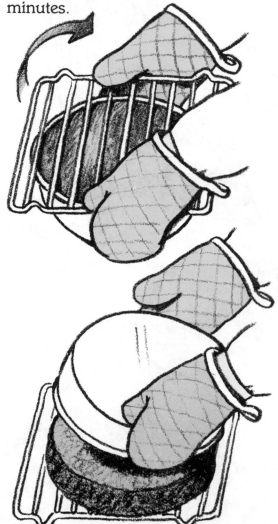

12 To serve, put the serving plate over the cake and turn the two over, so that the cake is right side up on the plate. Cut the cake into wedges and serve with whipped cream if you want.

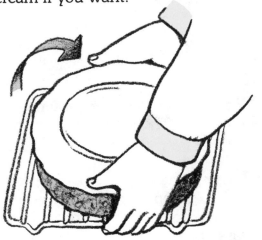

Tip: To make cracker crumbs, place the crackers in a brown paper bag. Fold the bag closed and set it on the counter. Using a rolling pin, roll over the bag several times until the crackers become crumbs.

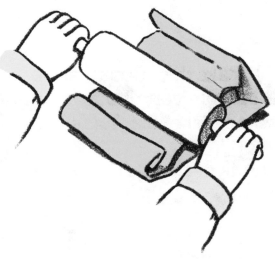

Apple Almond Tea Cake

Preparation time: 35 minutes
Baking time: 50 minutes
Makes: 18 servings

Make this special cake as your contribution to the school bake sale. You'll sell enough pieces to add a nice chunk of change to the kitty.

5¢ a piece

INGREDIENTS

½ cup (1 stick) butter, plus 2 teaspoons for the pan, at room temperature

2 cups all-purpose flour

1½ teaspoons baking powder

½ teaspoon ground nutmeg

½ cup granulated sugar

2 large eggs

1 cup milk

1 cup sliced almonds

2 medium apples

½ tablespoon brown sugar

½ teaspoon ground cinnamon

GLAZE:

3 tablespoons juice-sweetened apricot jam

1 tablespoon water

UTENSILS

Paper towel • 13 x 9-inch baking pan • Measuring cups and spoons • Small mixing bowl • Mixer bowl • Electric mixer • Rubber spatula • Cutting board • Vegetable peeler • Utility knife • Teaspoon • Oven mitts • Cooling rack • Small saucepan • Wooden spoon • Spoon • Metal spatula

1 Place an oven rack in the center of the oven. Then turn on the oven and preheat to 350°F.

2 Using the paper towel, spread the 2 teaspoons of butter evenly over the bottom and sides of the baking pan.

3 Put the flour, baking powder, and nutmeg in the small mixing bowl and stir them together with your fingers or a fork.

4 Put the ½ cup of butter and the granulated sugar in the mixer bowl. Using the electric mixer, beat on high speed until pale yellow and creamy. Stop every once in a while to scrape the sides of the bowl clean with the rubber spatula.

5 Break the eggs into the butter mixture and beat until blended.

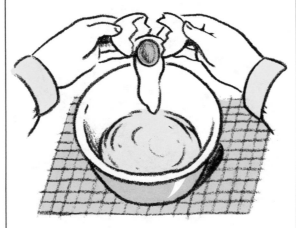

6 Add the flour mixture and mix on low speed until smooth.

7 Pour in the milk and mix again until smooth.

8 Using the rubber spatula, stir the almonds into the batter so they are completely covered with batter.

9 Scrape the batter into the prepared pan and spread evenly.

10 Put 1 apple on the cutting board. Holding the apple steady, peel the skin off the apple with the vegetable peeler.

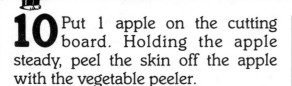
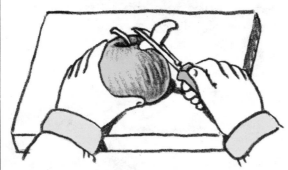

Carefully cut the apple in half through the stem end and center of the core. Repeat this with the other apple. Then, holding each apple half in the palm of your hand, scoop out the seeds and core with a teaspoon or metal teaspoon measure.

11 Turn the halves cut sides down on the cutting board. Using the utility knife, cut each half into thin slices.

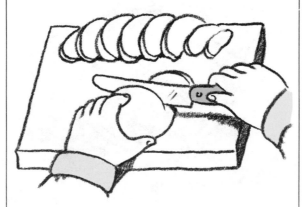

Arrange the apple slices in 3 long lines on top of the batter.

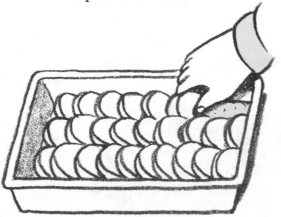

12 Mix the brown sugar and cinnamon in the small mixing bowl and sprinkle it over the apples and batter.

13 Put the oven mitts on and put the cake in the oven. Bake until the cake pulls away slightly from the sides of the pan, 50 minutes.

14 Wearing the mitts, carefully transfer the pan to the cooling rack. Let the cake cool for about 15 minutes.

15 While the cake is cooling, make the glaze: Place the jam in the saucepan.

Stir in the water with the wooden spoon and melt over medium heat.

When the jam melts and bubbles, put the oven mitts on and transfer the saucepan to a heatproof surface. Use the back of the spoon to spread the glaze over the cake.

16 To serve, cut the cake into 3 strips lengthwise and 6 strips crosswise. Use the metal spatula to slide the cake squares out of the pan and onto plates.

Custard Cups

Preparation time: 25 minutes
Baking time: 40 to 50 minutes
Makes: 8 servings

Nothing is more comforting than a creamy custard cup. Baking these is a sure way to beat the winter blues.

INGREDIENTS

3 large eggs

3 large egg yolks (see page 10 for separating eggs)

3 cups milk

¼ cup (packed) brown sugar

1½ teaspoons vanilla extract

1 tablespoon granulated sugar

½ teaspoon ground cinnamon

UTENSILS

8 ovenproof coffee cups or custard ramekins • 13 x 9-inch baking pan • Whisk • Small and medium-size mixing bowls • Measuring cups and spoons • Medium-size saucepan • Oven mitts • Cooling rack

1 Place an oven rack in the center of the oven. Then turn on the oven and preheat to 350°F.

2 Arrange the coffee cups in the baking pan.

3 Whisk the eggs and egg yolks together in the mixing bowl until blended. Pour in 1 cup milk and whisk until smooth.

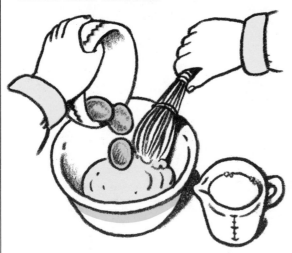

4 Pour the remaining 2 cups milk into the saucepan. Heat over medium heat until scalded (it steams and little bubbles form around the edge of the pan). Turn the heat off.

5 Put on an oven mitt and, holding the pan, add the brown sugar and vanilla to the milk and whisk until the sugar is dissolved.

Slowly pour in the egg mixture, while whisking constantly.

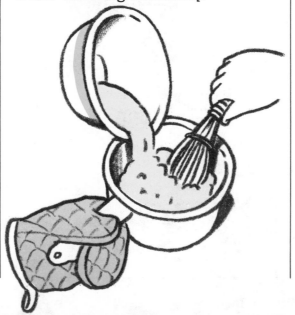

6 Pour 1 cup of the milk mixture into each cup.

7 Put the oven mitts on and put the pan in the oven. Bake 40 minutes. With your oven mitts on, test the custard for doneness. Gently shake one of the cups. If the custard is solid, it is done. If it is still loose, bake for another 10 minutes.

8 Wearing the mitts, carefully transfer the pan to the cooling rack. Mix the sugar and cinnamon together in the small mixing bowl. Sprinkle the custards with granulated sugar and cinnamon and let them cool slightly before serving.

Puffed Explosions

Preparation time: 30 minutes
Baking time: 40 minutes
Makes: 12 puffs

These are puffed balloons made with *choux* (pronounced SHOO) paste, which is a French batter for making cream puffs. Fill them with a special pudding or custard, and your friends' eyes will grow as big with delight as the puffs themselves!

INGREDIENTS

½ cup water
6 tablespoons butter
¾ cup all-purpose flour
4 large eggs
Vanilla Cream (recipe follows)

UTENSILS

Measuring cups and spoons • Medium-size saucepan • Oven mitts • Wooden spoon • Rubber spatula • Mixer bowl • Electric mixer • 2 nonstick cookie sheets • Kitchen scissors

1 Put the water and butter in the saucepan. Place the pan on a burner and turn the heat to medium-high. Heat until the water boils and all the butter melts.

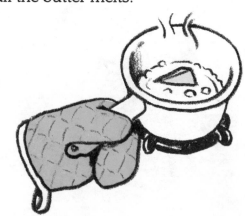

2 Put an oven mitt on for holding the pot and, with an adult's assistance, measure the flour into the water mixture and stir with the wooden spoon until it looks like a smooth, stiff paste. Turn the heat off and scrape the paste into the mixer bowl with the rubber spatula.

3 Break 2 eggs into the paste. Using the electric mixer, beat on

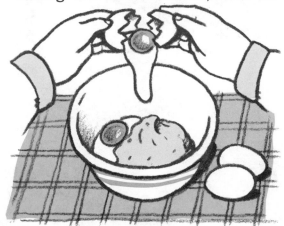

medium-high speed until completely blended. Break the remaining 2 eggs into the paste and beat again until blended.

4 Place an oven rack in the center of the oven. Then turn on the oven and preheat to 375°F.

5 Dip the teaspoon measure into cold water, then scoop out a spoonful of the paste and drop it onto a cookie sheet. Repeat, leaving 2 inches between spoonfuls of paste, until all the paste is gone.

6 Put on the oven mitts and put the cookie sheets in the oven. Bake for 20 minutes. Turn the oven heat down to 325°F and bake 20 minutes longer.

7 While the puffs are baking, make the Vanilla Cream.

8 Wearing the mitts, carefully transfer the cookie sheets to a heatproof surface. Let the puffs cool for 20 minutes.

9 Using the scissors, snip off a ½-inch lid from the top of each cream puff and save the lids. Carefully pick out any stringy uncooked dough from the inside of the puffs.

10 Spoon the vanilla cream into the puffs.

Put the lids back on the top of each puff. Serve the puffs as soon as you can.

Did You Know?

The water turning to steam is what makes these puffs puff.

Vanilla Cream

Preparation time: 15 minutes
Cooking time: 10 minutes
Makes: 3 cups

INGREDIENTS

5 tablespoons cornstarch

2 cups milk

2 large whole eggs

2 large egg yolks (see page 10 for separating eggs)

¼ cup sugar

1 teaspoon vanilla extract

UTENSILS

Measuring cups and spoons • Medium-size mixing bowl • Whisk • Medium-size saucepan • Oven mitt • Wooden spoon

1 Put the cornstarch in the mixing bowl. Add ½ cup of the milk and whisk until blended. Add the eggs and egg yolks and whisk again until blended.

2 Pour the remaining 1½ cups milk into the saucepan. Add the sugar and vanilla. Put the pan on a burner and turn the heat to medium-high.

Put on the oven mitt for holding the pot and heat, stirring occasionally with the wooden spoon, until sim-

mering (small bubbles will break on the top). Immediately turn the heat down to keep the milk at a slow simmer.

3 With an adult's assistance, slowly pour the egg mixture into the milk while whisking constantly with one hand. Keep whisking until the custard starts to boil. Then transfer the pan to a heatproof surface and whisk until the custard is cool.

"The Big Cheese" Cake

Preparation time: 40 minutes
Baking time: 20 minutes
Makes: 10 individual cheesecakes

There won't be any arguments about who has the biggest piece of cake. Everyone's the big cheese with these!

INGREDIENTS

CRUST:

¼ cup (½ stick) butter, plus 1 tablespoon for buttering the tin

¾ cup graham cracker crumbs (8 whole graham crackers; see Tip, page 111)

FILLING:

1 lemon

1 pound (two 8-ounce packages) cream cheese, at room temperature

⅓ cup sugar, plus additional for sprinkling over the tops

2 large eggs

¼ cup heavy cream

UTENSILS

Paper towel • 12-cup muffin tin • Measuring cups and spoons • Medium-size saucepan • Oven mitts • Wooden spoon • Grater • Aluminum foil • Mixer bowl • Electric mixer • Spoon • Large flat platter • Wide metal spatula

1 Place an oven rack in the center of the oven. Then turn on the oven and preheat to 350°F. Using the paper towel, coat 10 of the muffin cups lightly with 1 tablespoon of butter.

2 Make the crust: Put ¼ cup butter in the saucepan. Put the pan on a burner and turn the heat to medium. Heat until the butter is almost completely melted.

Put on the oven mitts for holding the pot and transfer it to a heatproof surface and let the butter cool a little.

3 Add the cracker crumbs to the melted butter and stir with the wooden spoon until all the crumbs are moistened.

4 Spoon the crumbs into the muffin cups, dividing them equally.

Press the crumbs evenly over the bottom of each cup with your fingers.

5 Make the filling: Put the grater on a small sheet of aluminum foil. Carefully grate the lemon zest (the colored part of the lemon peel) on the smallest holes of the grater. Be sure to keep turning the lemon so that none of the bitter white pith gets grated with the zest. Turn the grater over and scrape off the zest on the underside of the grater too.

6 Put the cream cheese and ½ cup sugar in the mixer bowl. Using the electric mixer, beat on medium speed until very creamy and smooth.

Break the eggs into the bowl and beat until completely blended. Pour in the cream and add the lemon zest. Beat again until blended. Pour or spoon the mixture evenly into the 10 muffin cups.

7 Put the oven mitts on and put the muffin tin in the oven. Bake until the centers of the cakes are firm, about 20 minutes. To test the cakes for doneness, gently shake the pan (with your oven mitts on). If the centers shake, bake for another 5 minutes.

8 Wearing the mitts, carefully transfer the tin to the cooling rack. Let the cakes cool for 20 minutes.

9 Sprinkle the tops of the cakes with sugar. (This will keep them from sticking during the next step.)

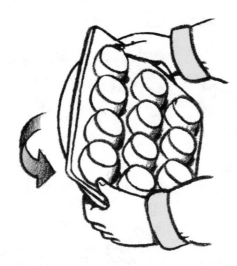

Place the platter upside down over the top of the tin. With an adult's assistance, hold the platter and the tin together and flip them over in one very quick motion, letting the cheesecakes drop onto the platter.

Lift the muffin tin off the cakes. Slide the spatula under each cake and turn it over so that it's right side up again.

Did You Know?

Cheesecake originated in New York City. Now nearly every deli and restaurant in New York has cheesecake on its menu, and they all claim to have the best and most famous one.

Apple Charlotte

Preparation time: 45 minutes
Baking time: 40 minutes
Makes: 1 Apple Charlotte (enough for 8)

A charlotte is really a special occasion dessert. Plan on baking it next time your grandparents come for a visit or for your parents' anniversary.

INGREDIENTS

12 slices white bread
¼ cup (½ stick) butter, at room temperature
3 apples
1 jar (23 ounces) unsweetened applesauce
½ teaspoon ground cinnamon
1 tablespoon quick-cooking tapioca
1 teaspoon vanilla extract
½ cup vanilla yogurt

UTENSILS

Toaster • Cutting board • Knife • 1½ quart casserole • Vegetable peeler • Teaspoon • Medium-size mixing bowl • Measuring cups and spoons • Oven mitts • Cookie sheet • Cooling rack

1 Place an oven rack in the center of the oven. Then turn on the oven and preheat to 350°F.

2 Toast the bread. Place the toasted slices on the cutting board and, using the knife, trim the crusts off of each slice. (See Tip.)

3 Spread the butter evenly over 1 side of each bread slice. Mold 9 of the bread slices around the bottom and side of the casserole dish with the buttered sides against the casserole. Tear pieces of the bread to fill in any holes around the casserole. Set the casserole aside.

4 Put 1 apple on the cutting board. Holding it steady, peel the skin off the apple with the vegetable peeler.

Carefully cut the apple in half through the stem end and center of the core. Repeat this with the other 2 apples. Holding each half in the palm of your hand, scoop out the seeds and the core with a teaspoon or metal teaspoon measure.

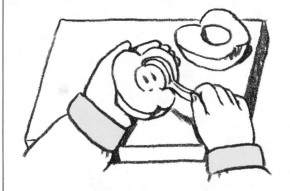

Turn the apple halves cut side down on the cutting board. Cut the apple into thin slices.

5 Place the applesauce in the mixing bowl. Add the cinnamon, tapioca, and vanilla.

Using the wooden spoon, stir until the cinnamon has disappeared into the applesauce. Add the apple slices and stir them into the mixture.

6 Pour the applesauce mixture into the bread-lined casserole. Arrange the remaining 3 bread slices on top of the apple mixture, keeping the buttered sides up.

7 Put on the oven mitts and place the cookie sheet in the oven. This casserole is heavy, so with an adult's assistance carefully place the casserole on the cookie sheet and bake until the bread pulls away from the side of the casserole, about 40 minutes.

8 Ask your adult assistant to re-move the casserole from the oven for you (besides being very heavy, now it will be very hot) and transfer it to a cooling rack. Let the charlotte cool for 20 minutes.

9 Unmold the charlotte with an adult's assistance (and with the oven mitts on). Put a plate on top of the casserole.

Quickly flip the casserole and plate over. Set it on the counter. Slowly lift the casserole straight off the char-lotte.

10 Eat the charlotte warm or cooled. Top it with a spoonful of yogurt.

Tip: Make the crusts into bread crumbs and use them to feed the birds next time you go to the park.

Austrian Soufflé

Preparation time: 25 minutes
Baking time: 15 minutes
Makes: 6 servings

This soufflé is the specialty from a small town in the Austrian Alps called Salzburg. The milk is soaked up by the soufflé while it bakes, creating a cream custard inside.

INGREDIENTS

1 cup milk

½ teaspoon vanilla extract

4 large eggs, at room temperature

½ cup (1 stick) butter, at room temperature

3 tablespoons granulated sugar

4 tablespoons all-purpose flour

2 teaspoons confectioner's sugar (optional)

UTENSILS

Measuring cups and spoons • Small saucepan • Oven mitts • 2 small and 1 large mixing bowls • Mixer bowl • Electric mixer • Rubber spatula • 9-inch cake pan • Hot pad

1 Place an oven rack in the center of the oven. Then turn on the oven and preheat to 350°F.

2 Put the milk and vanilla in the small saucepan. Heat over medium-high heat until scalded (it steams and small bubbles form around the edge of the pan). Put on an oven mitt and remove the pan from the heat. Place it on a heatproof surface for now.

3 Separate the eggs (see page 10) into the 2 small mixing bowls.

4 Put the butter in the mixer bowl. Using the electric mixer, beat on high speed until creamy. Add 2 tablespoons granulated sugar and beat until blended.

5 Add the egg yolks and mix on medium speed until smooth. Add 2 tablespoons flour and mix on low speed until completely blended. Scrape the butter mixture into the large mixing bowl with the rubber spatula.

6 Wash and dry the mixer bowl and beater. Pour the egg whites into the mixer bowl. Beat on high speed until very white and they hold a soft peak. On high speed, gradually beat in the remaining 2 tablespoons granulated sugar. Continue to beat until the whites are shiny and stiff. When the beater is lifted, the peak should not fall.

7 Sprinkle the remaining 2 tablespoons flour over the egg whites. Using the rubber spatula, fold in the flour by gently moving the spatula through the egg whites from the bottom of the bowl to the top and then down again.

8 Scrape the egg whites over the butter mixture and fold them gently together with the spatula.

9 Pour the warm milk into the cake pan, then scrape the soufflé batter on to the milk. Don't stir or spread the batter.

10 Put the oven mitts on and put the pan in the oven. Bake until the top is golden brown, about 15 minutes.

11 Wearing the oven mitts, carefully transfer the pan to the hot pad. Sprinkle the confectioner's sugar over the top, if you are using it, and serve the soufflé right away.

FIRST PRIZE

131

Washington's Cherry Tree

Preparation time: 45 minutes
Baking time: 15 minutes
Makes: 8 servings

If George Washington had this recipe, he wouldn't have chopped down that legendary cherry tree.

INGREDIENTS

CAKE:

1 teaspoon butter for the pan

4 large eggs, at room temperature

2 tablespoons granulated sugar

3 tablespoons unsweetened cocoa powder

1 teaspoon vanilla extract

1 tablespoon confectioner's sugar, optional

Chocolate Pudding Frosting, optional (recipe follows)

FILLING:

1 can (16 ounces) pitted black cherries

1 cup Unsweetened Whipped Cream (see page 11)

UTENSILS

Paper towel • 15½ x 10½-inch jelly-roll pan • Waxed paper • Mixer bowl • Large and small mixing bowls • Measuring cups and spoons • Electric mixer • Rubber spatula • Oven mitts • Kitchen towel (not terry cloth) • Knife • Colander • Can opener • Long serving platter

1 Place an oven rack in the center of the oven. Then turn on the oven and preheat to 350°F.

2 Using the paper towel, spread some of the butter over the bottom of the jelly-roll pan. Cut a piece of waxed paper to fit the bottom of the pan and put it on the butter. Spread more butter over the waxed paper.

3 Separate the eggs (see page 10), putting the egg yolks in the mixer bowl and the egg whites in the small mixing bowl.

4 Add the granulated sugar to the egg yolks. Using the electric mixer, beat on high speed until pale yellow and creamy. Sprinkle the cocoa over the egg yolks and add the vanilla; beat until blended.

Scrape the chocolate mixture into the large mixing bowl with the rubber spatula. Wash and dry the mixer bowl and beater.

5 Put the egg whites in the mixer bowl. Using the electric mixer, beat on medium-high speed until they are very white and they hold a peak when the beater is lifted up (with the mixer turned off).

6 Using the rubber spatula, scrape the egg whites over the chocolate mixture.

Fold in the egg whites by gently moving the spatula through the mixture from the bottom of the bowl to the top and then down again. Keep folding until all the egg whites have disappeared into the chocolate.

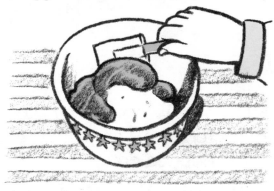

7 Scrape the batter onto the prepared pan and spread it evenly over the pan.

8 Put the oven mitts on and put the pan in the oven. Bake until the cake pulls away slightly from the sides of the pan, 15 minutes.

9 While the cake is baking, spread a kitchen towel on a clean kitchen surface and sprinkle it evenly with the confectioner's sugar, if you are using it.

10 Wearing the mitts and with an adult's assistance, carefully remove the pan from the oven and gently turn it upside down onto the towel. Take the pan off the cake. Let the cake cool for 10 minutes.

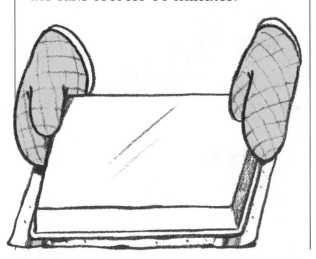

11 Gently peel off the waxed paper. If the cake sticks to the paper, carefully scrape it off the paper with the knife.

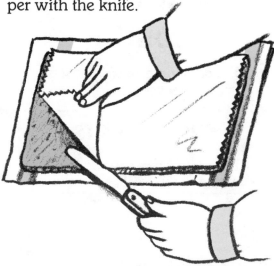

12 Make the filling: Put the colander in the sink. Open the can of cherries with the can opener and pour them into the colander to drain.

13 Using the knife, spread the whipped cream evenly over the cake. Arrange the cherries on the cream.

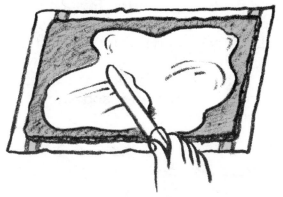

14 Starting at one long side of the cake and using the towel to lift the cake, roll up the cake as tightly as possible. Wrap the cake in the towel and put it on the serving platter. Refrigerate the cake until you are ready to frost it or serve it.

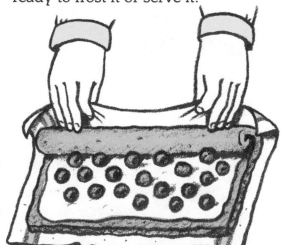

15 If you want to frost the cake, make Chocolate Pudding Frosting (recipe follows). Gently ease the cake out of the towel and onto the platter. Spread the frosting over the cake with a table knife or spatula. If you don't want to frost it, sprinkle confectioner's sugar over the cake. Cut a thin slice off each end of the log to neaten it and bring the platter to the table.

Chocolate Pudding Frosting

Preparation time: 5 minutes
Makes: 1 cup

INGREDIENTS

⅓ cup semisweet chocolate chips

3 tablespoons cornstarch

1 cup warm water

½ teaspoon vanilla extract

2 tablespoons butter

UTENSILS

Measuring cups and spoons • Medium saucepan • Wire whisk • Oven mitt • Hot pad

1 Put the chocolate chips, and cornstarch in the saucepan. Put the pan on the stove and pour in the warm water. Stir well with the whisk, then turn the heat to medium-high. Put on the oven mitt, and holding the handle of the pan, whisk constantly until the mixture is thick and smooth.

2 Place the pan on the hot pad. Add the vanilla and butter and whisk until the butter is melted into the frosting, 10 minutes.

3 Spread the warm frosting over the cake.

Fall Harvest Apple and Cheddar Pie

Preparation time: 1 hour   Baking time: 55 minutes   Makes: 8-inch pie

As American as apple pie? Wrong! Apple pie came from England with the pilgrims in 1630. It becomes American by adding the Cheddar cheese.

INGREDIENTS

DOUGH:

2 cups all-purpose flour, plus 3 to 4 tablespoons for rolling out the dough

½ teaspoon salt

⅔ cup solid vegetable shortening

⅓ cup cold water

FILLING:

4 baking apples

⅔ cup grated mild Cheddar cheese

½ cup coarsely chopped walnuts

2 tablespoons sugar

1 tablespoon quick-cooking tapioca

½ teaspoon ground cinnamon

GLAZE:

1 large egg

1 tablespoon water

UTENSILS

Measuring cups and spoons • Large mixing bowl • Plastic wrap • Cutting board • Vegetable peeler • Knife • Teaspoon • Grater • Waxed paper • Wooden spoon • Rolling pin • Ruler • 9-inch pie plate • Knife • Fork • Small bowl • Pastry brush • Cookie sheet • Oven mitts • Cooling rack

1 Make the dough: Place 2 cups flour and the salt in the mixing bowl and stir them together with your fingers. Add the shortening and rub the shortening and flour together between your fingertips until all the shortening disappears into the flour.

2 Sprinkle the cold water over the flour mixture. Toss the flour and water together with your hands until all the flour is moistened and the dough comes together.

Shape the dough into a ball, then flatten it, wrap it in a piece of plastic wrap, and refrigerate it for about 15 minutes.

3 Make the filling: Put 1 apple on the cutting board. Holding the apple steady, peel the skin off with the vegetable peeler.

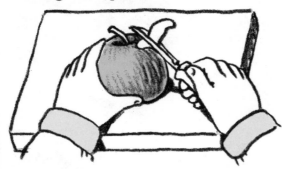

Carefully cut the apple in half through the stem end and center of the core. Repeat this with the other 3 apples. Holding each apple half in the palm of your hand, scoop out the seeds and core with the teaspoon or metal teaspoon measure.

Turn the apple halves cut side down on the cutting board and cut into thin slices. Put all the slices in the mixing bowl.

4 Place the grater on top of a piece of waxed paper. Using the largest holes, grate the cheese, watching carefully so that you do not scrape your fingers. You should have about ⅔ cup of cheese.

5 Add the cheese, walnuts, sugar, tapioca, and cinnamon to the apples and stir them together with the wooden spoon.

6 Place an oven rack in the center of the oven. Then turn on the oven and preheat to 350°F.

7 Sprinkle a clean kitchen surface with a little flour. Break the dough in half. Place 1 piece on the floured surface; rewrap the other piece and return it to the refrigerator.

Lightly dust the dough with flour and press it flat with your hands. Using the rolling pin, roll out the dough ¼ inch thick (see page 11).

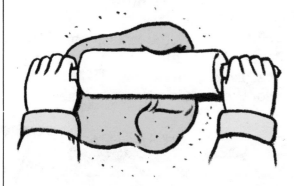

Place the pie plate over the dough and check to see that the dough is large enough to line the plate.

Gently lift and fold the dough in half, and then in half again. Unfold it over the plate. Press the dough lightly into the pie plate.

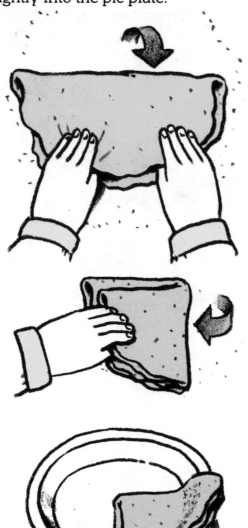

8 Stir the apple mixture and spoon it evenly into the pie plate.

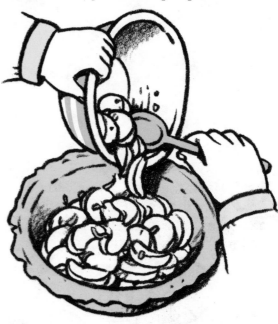

9 Roll out the second piece of dough the same way. Gently lift and fold it in half. Unfold it over the filling. Using the knife, trim the excess dough around the edge.

Press the edges of the dough together around the rim with the fork.

10 Make the glaze: Break the egg into the small bowl and add the water. Stir them together with the fork.

Using the pastry brush or your fingers, brush the egg glaze over the top of the pie. (You'll have more glaze than you need. Save it for making scrambled eggs if you want.) If you want, write your initials in the glaze with the table knife.

11 Put the oven mitts on and put the cookie sheet in the oven. Place the pie plate on the cookie sheet. Bake until the pastry is golden brown, 45 to 55 minutes.

12 Wearing the mitts, carefully remove the pie to the cooling rack. Let it cool at least 15 minutes before serving it.

INDEX